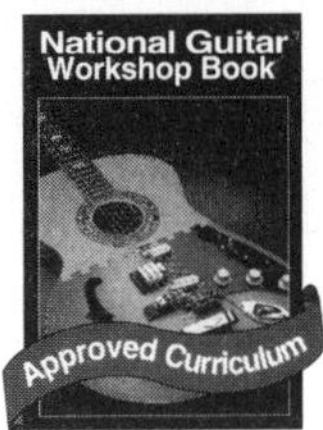

Technique-Building Exercises You Can Do While Watching TV!

GREG HORNE

Alfred, the leader in educational music publishing, and the National Guitar Workshop, one of America's finest guitar schools, have joined forces to bring you the best, most progressive educational tools possible. We hope you will enjoy this book and encourage you to look for other fine products from Alfred and the National Guitar Workshop.

This book was acquired, edited, and produced by Workshop Arts, Inc., the publishing arm of the National Guitar Workshop.

Nathaniel Gunod, acquisitions, managing editor
Burgess Speed, acquisitions, senior editor
Timothy Phelps, interior design
Ante Gelo, music typesetter
Barbara Smolover, illustrator

Interior and cover photographs: © Paige M. Travis
Visit her blog: www.rocknrollsoapbox.com

Cover illustration: Stick Figure © iStockphoto.com / Toby Bridson

Alfred Music Publishing Co., Inc.
P.O. Box 10003
Van Nuys, CA 91410-0003
alfred.com

ISBN-10: 0-7390-7546-2
ISBN-13: 978-0-7390-7546-3

CONTENTS

ABOUT THE AUTHOR

Greg Horne is a bassist, guitarist, songwriter, author, and teacher in Knoxville, Tennessee. He is a senior faculty member of the National Guitar Workshop, and author of several books and DVDs published by National Guitar Workshop and Alfred, including the *Complete Acoustic Guitar Method*, *Teach Yourself Songwriting*, and two volumes of the *Complete Mandolin Method*. Greg holds a bachelor of arts in music from the College of Wooster and pursued graduate studies at the University of Mississippi.

Greg would like to thank editors Burgess Speed and Link Harnsberger for the great idea for this book. As a fan of both potatoes and couches, Greg does some of his practicing while watching reruns of '70s sitcoms and thinking about sweet potato fries.

To contact Greg, hear his music, and see his videos, please visit: www.greghornemusic.com

INTRODUCTION

Welcome to *The Couch Potato Bass Workout*. This page has a lot of text on it, so you might want to read it while you're microwaving popcorn or something.

WHO IS THIS BOOK FOR?

Players of all levels—beginning to advanced—can benefit from the exercises and information in this book. It is helpful if you already know how to read standard notation or TAB, but if you do not, there is a review starting on page 6. It is also helpful if you already have a grasp of basic bass guitar technique. But if you don't, you will find plenty of helpful tips throughout.

HOW TO USE THIS BOOK

Mixed in with all the silliness in this book are some good tips about how your hands work, how to practice, and how to achieve real improvement. The exercises in this book are meant to give you ideas that you can build on as your technique improves. It's an idea book. There isn't a set program of exercises to follow, because everybody has different problems to solve and different goals.

Exercises are solutions to problems. For an exercise to do any good, you have to know what problem you're trying to solve. You'll get the most benefit by using a small number of exercises and practicing them over the course of several sessions. Improvement will be gradual, and the process is helped by working on something for a while, letting it rest, and trying it again at the next session. Again, the "rest" part is important. When an exercise isn't showing results after a while, flip through the book and find a new one to add to the mix. Try to find things that relate to other stuff you're practicing when you're not on the couch.

ABOUT BASS LEFT-HAND FINGERING

There are multiple schools of thought about left-hand fingering on the bass, specifically regarding the notes in the lower positions. This book will generally follow the one-finger-per-fret method (or, "1–2–3–4"). Many of the exercises will be shown starting in higher positions to facilitate this fingering with ease. If you use the Simandl* fingering of 1-2-4 on the lower frets (or some variation), you can easily adapt these exercises. It is possible for highly repetitive exercises to cause stress or damage if practiced without good technique. A qualified teacher can help you determine the best fingering method and hand position for you and your bass.

IT'S ALL A TRICK, MWAHAHAHA!

The truth is that you can't be totally mindless when you're doing technique-building exercises. You have to be paying attention to what you're doing, how you're doing it, and why you're doing it in the first place. At first, it would be smart to do your couch potato exercises during commercials with the sound off so you can really focus. After you get a repertoire of exercises mastered, you'll have a better technical foundation when you want to just zone out and hammer away at those bass strings.

The main thing is to build better playing habits, rather than add more bad habits. Listen to your tone, observe the feelings in your muscles and joints, stay relaxed and try to make as good of a sound as you possibly can.

HIDDEN BENEFITS

Sitting on the couch ranks low on doctor-recommended methods of weight loss. Nevertheless, it just might be beneficial to grab your bass and dash off a few finger twisters the next time the pizza delivery commercial beckons you with its hypnotic cheesy charms. An arpeggio learned is another pizza crisis averted.

---

* Franz Simandl (1840–1912) was a double bassist, teacher, and author of the book *New Method for the Double Bass*.

HOW TO SIT ON A COUCH AND A FEW SAFETY TIPS

You would think this is the easy part, wouldn't you?

Seriously, though, most of us sit on couches as if the bones that hold us up had all turned into lo mein—not the best guitar playing position. Plus, couches are squishy. Your elbows and arms are probably going to bump into things like stacks of laundry, magazines, and that vacuum cleaner hose that got stuck behind the cushion.

If you're really hoping to get something out of the mindless exercises in this book, clear yourself some space on the mothership. Get your bass in a position that makes it easier to play, somewhat centered on the body with the headstock pointing more up than down. A strap may help, but you'll probably need to cinch it up higher than normal to do any good.

Get your arms, elbows, and hands into a position where they can move freely without having to bend your wrists at a sharp angle. You want to prevent repetitive stress injuries, which can sneak up on you when you're hammering your way through a cop show marathon.

If you're going to do some serious technique building (during commercials, of course), consider moving up to the edge of the sofa and sitting up straight with both feet on the floor. It will improve circulation, give you the most freedom of movement, and make it easier to reach that bag of microwave popcorn you forgot about yesterday.

Finally, if you must have your amp nearby, make sure it is stable and has plenty of ventilation. These exercises aren't that great for your neighbors to listen to anyway, so you'll save some fossil fuels and prevent fire risk by turning it off altogether. Besides, if it's too loud, you won't hear who got voted off the pontoon boat in your favorite reality show.

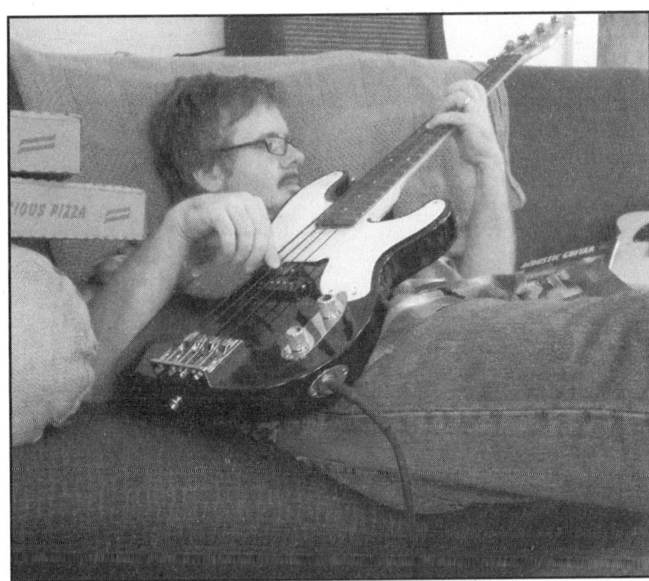

Bad arm position and posture.

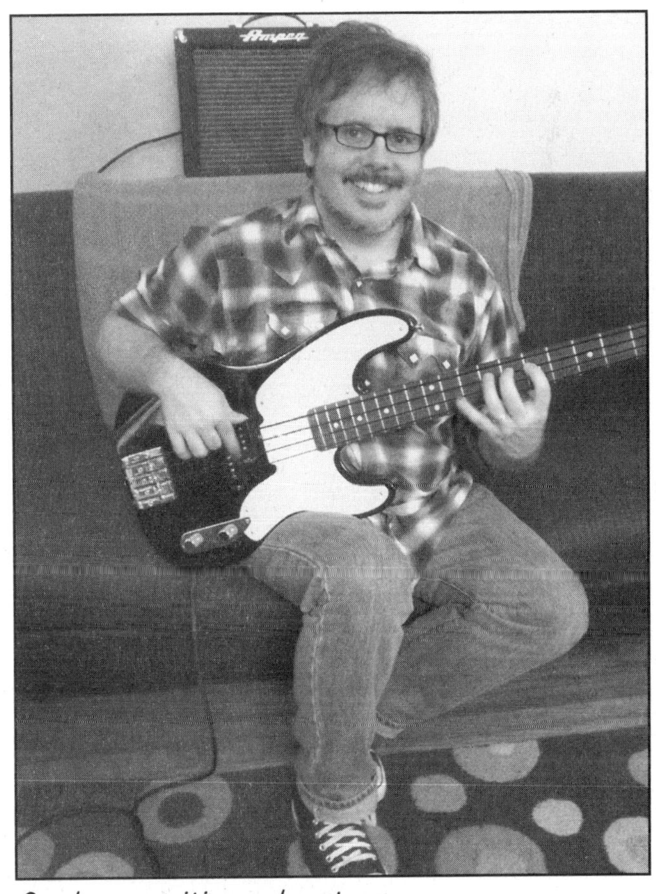

Good arm position and posture.

 # MUSIC NOTATION REVIEW 

If you see something you don't understand in an example in this book, check the following two pages.

TABLATURE (TAB)

TAB (short for *tablature*) is the easiest way to read bass music, though it leaves out some information about rhythm and expression. Here's what you might see on some TAB.

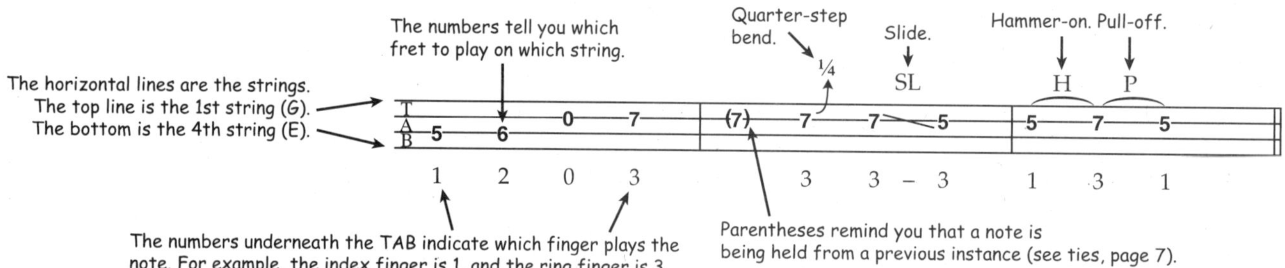

STANDARD MUSIC NOTATION

Standard music notation uses a *staff* of five horizontal lines to indicate *pitch* (the highness or lowness of a tone). Lower lines represent lower pitches. Notes are shown by oval *noteheads* o placed on lines, or in spaces between lines. Below are the basic notes on the staff. Notes are named "A" through "G."

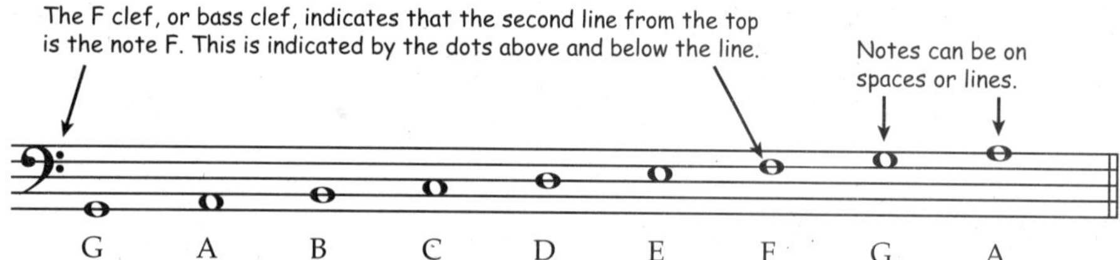

In this book, standard music notation is directly above the TAB staff.

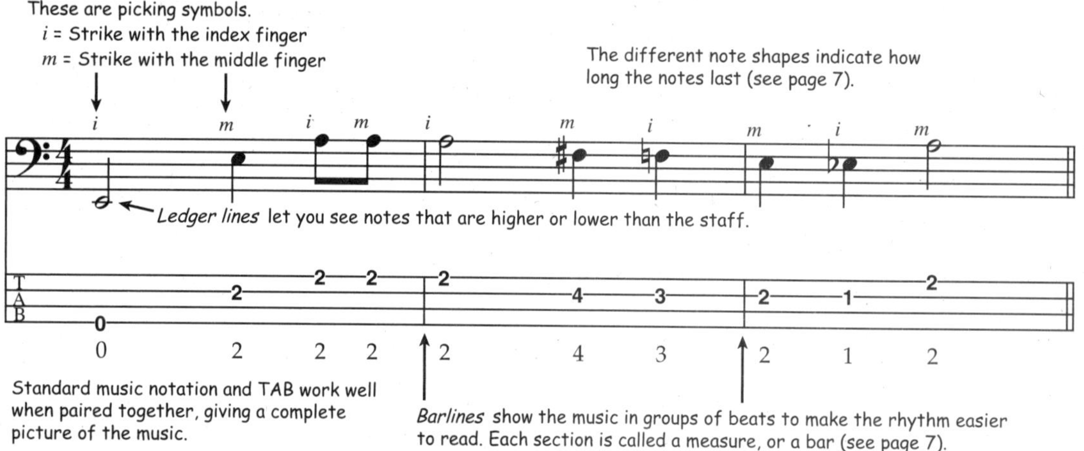

ACCIDENTALS

Accidentals are symbols used to change the pitch of a note.

♯ is a *sharp*. It raises a note one *half step* (one fret).

♭ is a *flat*. It lowers a note one half step.

A sharp or flat will last for the rest of the measure, unless a *natural* ♮ is used to return the note to its original pitch.

KEY SIGNATURES

Sharps or flats at the beginning of the staff are called the *key signature*. The key signature affects the indicated pitches in all octaves throughout the piece. To the right is the key signature for D Major, in which all F's and C's are sharped throughout.

RHYTHM NOTATION

Rhythm in music is organized around the *beat*, which is the basic, steady pulse of a piece of music. Beats are grouped in *measures*, which are also called *bars*. Each measure has an equal number of beats. At the beginning of a piece of music is the *time signature*, which consists of two numbers, one stacked on top of the other. The top number shows how many beats will be in each measure. The bottom number shows what kind of note will equal one beat. This is commonly a 4, representing the quarter note.

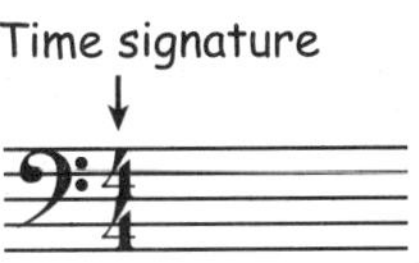

Notes are shown with different shapes to indicate their *value,* or duration, in beats or fractions of beats. Periods of silence in music are indicated with *rests*. Following are the note shapes and rests with their durations.

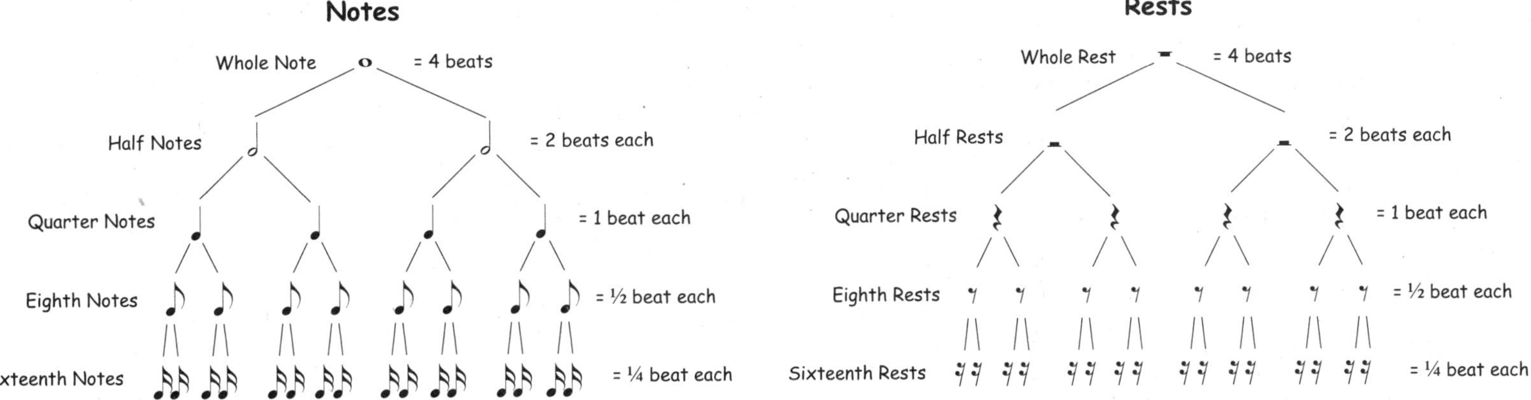

MORE RHYTHM SYMBOLS

A *dot* after a notehead increases the duration of the note by one half of its original value. This dotted half note lasts for 3 beats (2 + 1 = 3).

The left-facing repeat indicates a repeat of the passage of music. A right-facing repeat shows where to begin the repeated passage. If no right-facing repeat is shown, repeat from the beginning.

A *tie* connects two note values and makes them into one note lasting the duration of both. This note would last for 5 beats (4 + 1 = 5).

"SERIOUSLY, WHY DO YOU KEEP TWITCHING LIKE THAT?"— A LESSON IN FINGER MECHANICS

FLEXORS AND EXTENSORS

There are several different muscles that control finger movement. There are larger muscles in your forearm that connect to your fingers by tendons that travel through your wrist. There are also smaller muscles in your hand that control finer finger movements. This lesson concerns specific actions—*flexion, extension*, and the *twitch* response—in the larger muscles of your forearm.

Flexors pull the finger toward the palm. *Extensors* straighten the finger out or lift the finger up. Imagine yourself typing—flexors press a key down, extensors lift the finger off the key.

TWITCHY, TWITCHY, TWITCHY

When you're first learning, you engage strong muscles that employ force and power to hold down the strings, like the kind you use to make and hold a fist. Remember those days?

With experience, just pressing down the strings becomes less of a big deal, and you're able to work on agility. This is where *fast twitch* muscle responses come into play. The fast twitch is used to move a body part to a new location quickly with a single impulse. Athletes such as runners train the fast twitch muscles in their legs to aid in sprints.

For a musician, the twitch response makes all the difference in building agility while minimizing wear and tear (and possibly injury) to muscles and tendons. The first step is to identify the twitch so that you know what it feels like. Try the following:

1. **Achieve the resting point**

   Hold your fretting hand out in front of you, arm bent at the elbow as if you were looking at a wristwatch. Now, turn the back of your hand away from you about a quarter turn so you are looking at your thumb and index finger. Let the weight of your hand drop and relax, like you are floating in water. You are ready to get your flexor/extensor-twitch kung fu on. Take a deep breath, relax, and tune in to your body.

   First, observe that relaxed, floating-in-water state that your hand is hanging out in. This is the middle ground, the state of equilibrium between the flexors and extensors. It represents your finger when it is ready to play a note, but hasn't pressed down yet. This is the *resting point*.

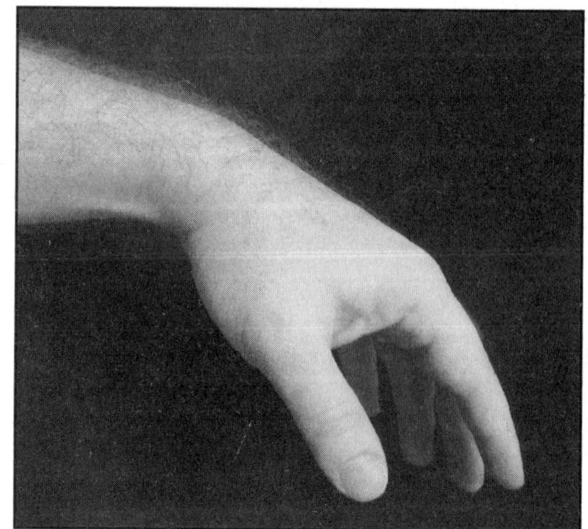

Resting point.

2. Do the flexor twitch

Twitch your index finger in toward your palm, as if you were scratching an itch just once. Your finger will travel a certain distance, beyond which you would have to engage other muscles to pull it all the way into your palm. We'll call this the *flexor twitch point*. Once you've twitched, you can either hold the finger in place at the twitch point (you might find it vibrates a little if you're really relaxed) or you can let it fall back to the resting point.

Twitch your index finger several times, letting it immediately fall back to the rest point. The movement should come from the knuckle where the finger joins the hand, not the joints further down the finger. This joint is called the *metacarpophalangeal* (or *MCP*) joint. If you're doing this right, you might actually feel the twitch ripple in the muscles of your forearm.

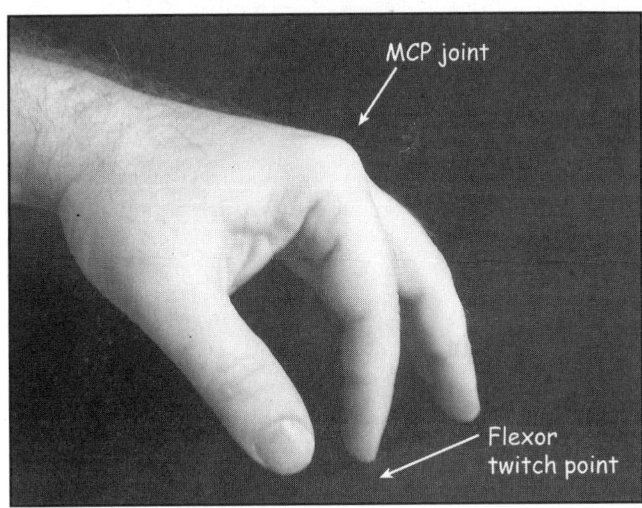

Flexor twitch point.

3. Do the extensor twitch

With your fingers in the resting point, try twitching your index finger the opposite direction, away from your palm. *Voila!* Extensor twitch! Let it fall back to the resting point. Try this twitch with other fingers. At first, you may have trouble isolating them. That's part of the process.

The extensor twitch is sometimes not as developed or practiced as the flexor twitch. Just remember that the extensor twitch is what gets your fretting finger off of a note and moving to the next one. It is just as important as the flexor twitch. Well developed extensor responses can make the difference between a flurry of distinct notes and an unsynchronized mess.

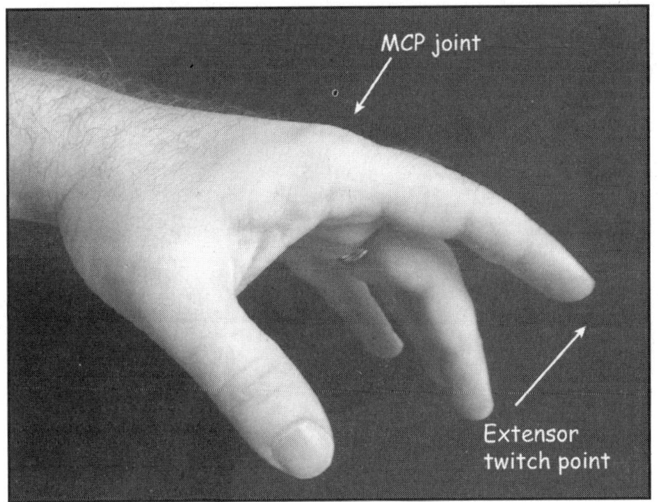

Extensor twitch point.

4. Try your other fingers

Congratulations, you have now isolated the flexor and extensor muscle twitch response; it's small, quick, and powerful. Try all your different fingers, even the fingers on your picking hand. If you are a fingerstyle player, you'll need those picking hand twitches just as much as the fretting ones.

You can practice isolating the twitch response anywhere anytime, without anybody really noticing too much. The more you practice it, the more control your brain has over those nerves and muscles. The ring finger and pinky need more practice than the others, they just aren't hooked up as well to the brain as the index finger and thumb.

FINGER MECHANICS MAXIMIZERS (OR, HOW TO PRACTICE WITHOUT DRIVING YOUR COUCHMATE BANANAS)

Though it is hard to believe now, sometimes you will want to share your couch with other, non-guitar obsessed people. These people may not appreciate your desire to use every waking moment for the good of your bass skills. They might just want to sit next to you and watch a movie or talk, or something like that. This kind of person is likely to fire you as their friend if they have to listen to hours of your "ticka-ticka-ticka" picking exercises every time they are trying to relax. Life is full of opportunities for compromise.

The good news is that a great deal of the value of practice consists of building the neural pathways that give your brain finer and more nimble control of your nervous system. Some of these pathways can be developed and strengthened even if someone has locked your bass in the closet until you can learn to show some respect for the couch potato ways of others.

These "stealth" exercises can be done anywhere at any time. They work for both hands, even simultaneously. The thumb moves in a different direction than the fingers (hooray for opposable thumbs!), so use a little common sense in adapting these exercises to the thumb. Let it go the direction it wants to go.

STEALTH EXERCISE NO. 1: THE TELEGRAPH OPERATOR

In a "typing" position, rest your fingertips on your leg (or some other surface that allows your arm and shoulder to be relaxed). Your forearm and palm should be floating (not resting on the surface), and your wrist should be straight or arched slightly up. With all the other fingertips still touching the surface, raise and lower one finger in a typing motion. Repeat the motion 10 or 20 times before moving to the next finger. Start out slow and then go faster if you want.

TIPS: Stay relaxed! This exercise is for agility, not force. It's also about isolating the fingers so that you can move them without affecting the relaxation of the remaining fingers. You'll probably find this to be hardest with the ring finger, so be patient with that one.

STEALTH EXERCISE NO. 2: THE MINIATURE CHORUS LINE

Where the Telegraph Operator exercise mostly worked the flexors, this one works the extensors. Start in the same relaxed, resting-on-your-fingertips position. Start with the index finger, making a sudden, quick-fire kicking motion up in the air, while the other fingertips stay down. Think extensor twitch. Let the finger fall back down to the rest state, you don't need to bring it down with any force. Do this 10–20 times with each finger, and cycle through the fingers as much as you want.

STEALTH EXERCISE NO. 3: THE AMATEUR DANCE TEAM

This is a variation on the first two exercises where you attempt to do the exercise with two or three fingers together. If you're "typing," try to make the fingers contact the surface exactly at the same time, generating a single tapping sound. It's harder than it seems. You could also try this with the fingertips floating slightly above the surface.

STEALTH EXERCISE NO. 4: THE PENDULUM

Again, with your fingertips resting on the surface and your wrist arched up slightly, lift up the index finger and curl it in slightly so the finger doesn't touch the surface. Swing the finger forward and back like a pendulum (toward the palm, then away). If it helps you to imagine your swinging finger as a giant axe blade swinging in a graceful yet menacing manner over some hapless victim in an old horror movie, by all means do so. Try with each finger.

STEALTH EXERCISE NO. 5: THE VENUS FLYTRAP AND THE LEAPING TARANTULA

Hold your hand and arm so they are not resting on a surface, just relaxed and floating. Practice suddenly firing your flexor twitches all at once so that your fingers close on your palm fast like a Venus Flytrap (or like you're trying to clap with only one hand). Do this 10 times, then rest for 10 seconds. This and the following exercises are great for when you're warming up to practice or perform.

The extensor twitch version of the flytrap is the leaping tarantula. Starting from the resting state, suddenly extend your fingers from the MCP joint, then let them fall back to rest. It should look a little like a spider that has been disturbed and has used all its legs at once to spring into the air. Sleeping cats do this sort of thing in cartoons.

STRETCHING IS GOOD FOR YOU

Stretches can be done before you practice, during a break in practice, and after you're done. Below are a few good ones. Be gentle, go slow, and allow them to develop over time.

STRETCH NO. 1

Place your palms together in front of you, with the fingers and palms touching but not pressed hard together. First, bring your fingers together, then spread them apart several times (still touching each other). Then, keeping your fingers touching, very slowly and gently raise your elbows so that your palms gradually separate. Hold the stretch for 10 or 15 seconds, then slowly release and repeat. Don't force this stretch to go farther than you are comfortable all at once.

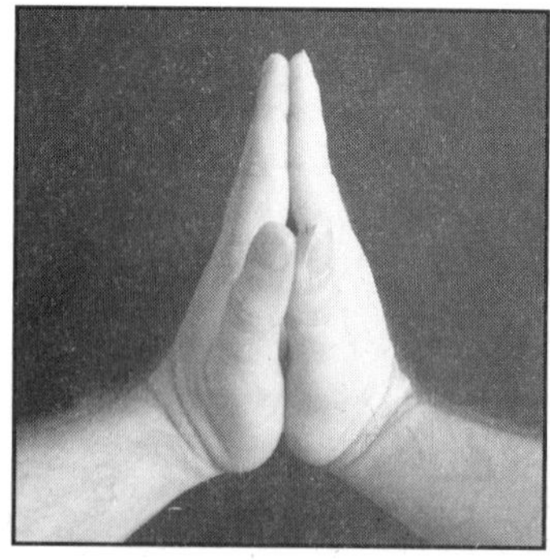 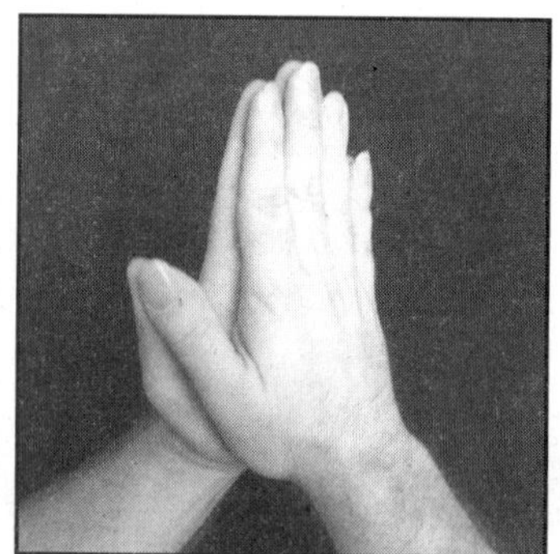 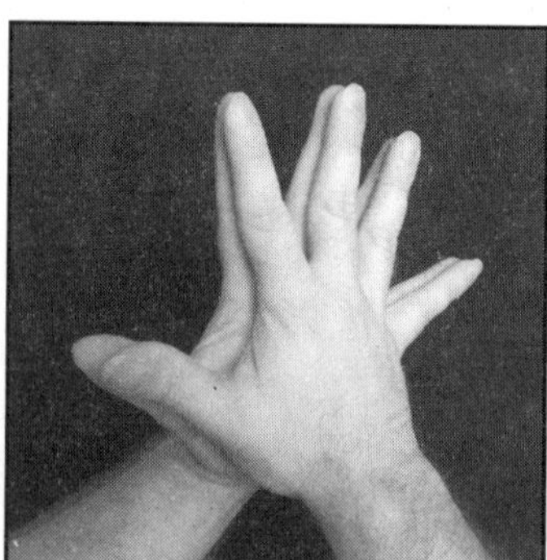 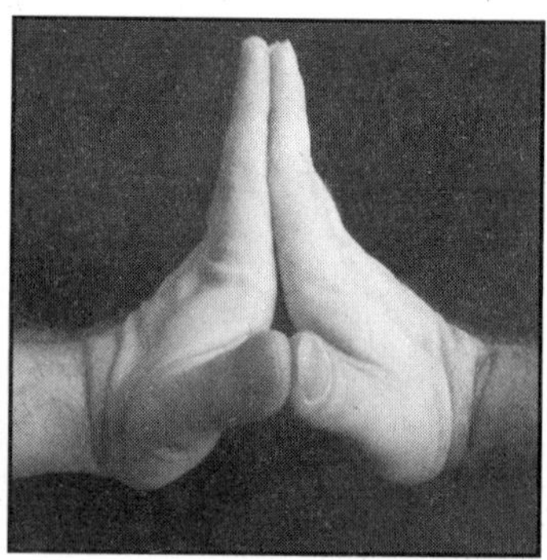

STRETCH NO. 2

Place the backs of your hands together in front of you, with the fingers hanging down. Slowly lower your elbows so that you feel a gentle stretch across the back of your wrists. Don't go too far. Hold for 10 or 15 seconds, slowly release, and repeat.

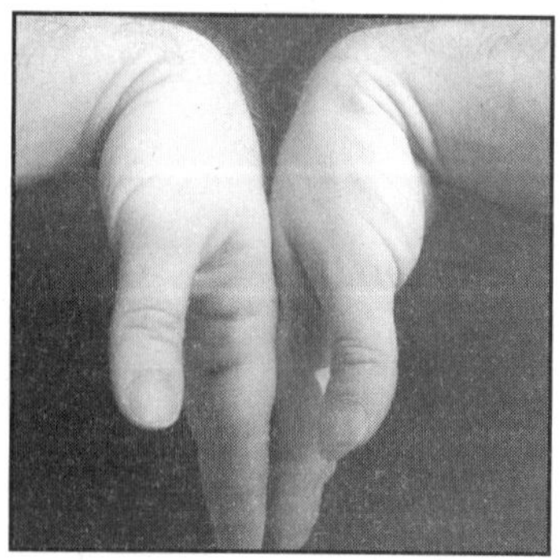

STRETCH NO. 3

You might need to stand up for this one. Hold your arms outstretched, parallel to the floor. Slowly make small circles with your arms going forward, and as you go, make the circles wider and wider. When your arms are almost vertical, begin making the circles smaller until you are back to the tiny circles you started with. Rest for a little while, then repeat with the circles going backward. This one is great for your shoulders and the circulation in your entire arm, which will improve the functioning of your fingers.

HEADROOM IS EVERYTHING

Imagine that your personal technique has three zones: easy, comfortably challenging, and redline. That redline zone is where things get uncomfortable and start to fall apart physically. It is the "ceiling" of your technique. Your goal with exercises and practice is to raise the ceiling, or to increase the *headroom* between the demands of the music you play and the ceiling of your ability to play. That headroom zone will be unique to the music and experience of each player. Here are a few simple guiding thoughts to keep in mind while practicing exercises.

THREE CONCEPTS THAT ARE ESSENTIAL TO HEADROOM

- **Accuracy**—A bunch of messy notes, when sped up, is a fast mess.
- **Synchronization** of right and left hand—The picking motion and the fretting motion need to be coordinated perfectly, or else you get missed notes.
- **Relaxation**—Learning to play without effort actually takes some effort. You have to think about and practice relaxing while you play.

Following are a few tips on the right and wrong approaches to practicing and increasing headroom.

THE WRONG WAY	THE RIGHT WAY
Practice incessantly, feel the burn.	Take breaks. Rest helps newly acquired skills become muscle memories (repeatable motions that don't have to be planned ahead).
Power through the pain.	Respond to pain by backing off, relaxing, taking a break, and examining your position to find the source of the problem. Reduce stress on your muscles, tendons, and joints whenever possible.
To play faster and faster, tighten up and force your way through.	Gradually, over a period of time, raise the speed at which you are able to play and still be relaxed.
Twist yourself into whatever position gets the job done.	Work on playing from as natural and relaxed a position as possible. Try to eliminate sharp bends in the wrist and arm, and tension in the neck and shoulders.
Move your picking and fretting fingers fast and one day it will come together.	Get your picking and fretting fingers perfectly synchronized first. Make good, clear tones while playing slowly, and try to maintain clarity and accuracy as the tempo increases.

# THE MOTHER OF ALL MINDLESS FRETBOARD EXERCISES

Here it is. It's as easy as one, two, three, four. Start at the 7th position (1st finger, 7th fret) on the 4th string. Starting higher up on the neck like this makes the one-finger-per-fret hand position easier to work with. When you finish on the 1st string, move up one fret position and begin again, working from the 1st string back to the 4th. Keep going up the neck. If you want to try it in lower positions, you may need to adapt the fingering or shift your hand position to stay comfortable. Learn this exercise using steady quarter notes (which are counted: "1, 2, 3, 4").

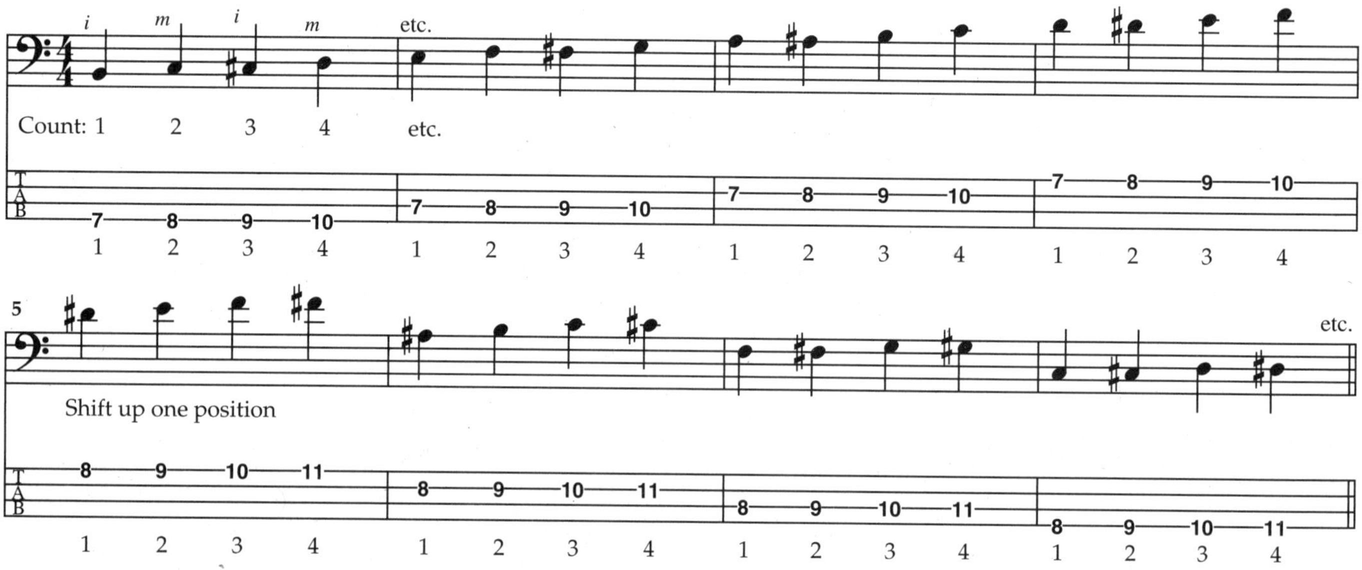

Once you get this exercise coordinated and can do it without having to stop and think about where to go next, it's time to bring in the *metronome!* This is an adjustable time-keeping device that clicks at a steady tempo, allowing you to regulate your speed, as well as increase it incrementally. If you don't have a metronome, get one, or get a metronome software app for the computer device of your choice.

THE "GOLDILOCKS" PRINCIPLE APPLIED TO SPEED BUILDING

In the kids' story of *Goldilocks and the Three Bears,* the fickle young diva Goldilocks tries three chairs. One is too hard, one is too soft, and one is just right. With that in mind, here's a three-stage approach to speed building using your trusty metronome.

1. **Practice too slow.** Set the metronome to a very slow speed and work on the exercise while focusing on timing, relaxation, and tone. Create the best-sounding notes you can at this stage.

2. **Practice too fast.** Find the highest metronome speed that still allows you to play the exercise perfectly. This is your *best fast speed.* For a short period of time, a few minutes or so, set the metronome a few clicks higher than your best fast speed. You won't be able to keep up perfectly, just relax and do the best you can. The purpose of this is to condition your brain to send the "playing instructions" to your muscles at a faster rate. It's okay if you don't have it perfect after a few minutes. Don't do this too long, or you may stress your muscles.

3. **Practice just right.** After you've practiced too fast for a little while, stop and rest a minute or so. Then dial the metronome back to the best fast speed you started with. Now, when you play at this speed, it should feel easier and more effortless than it did before. Gradually, over a period of days (or weeks or months), you'll find that your best fast speed keeps creeping its way up the metronome dial. Be patient. Your headroom is increasing!

If you can do the basic exercise perfectly and easily using quarter notes, it's time to try it with each note doubled in eighth notes. Eighth notes are counted: "1-&, 2-&, 3-&, 4-&." Continue using alternating *i* and *m* fingers to play the eighth notes. Try to make every note equal in tone and volume.

When you can work your way up the neck using double eighth notes, start doing the exercise with single eighth notes (still alternate picking).

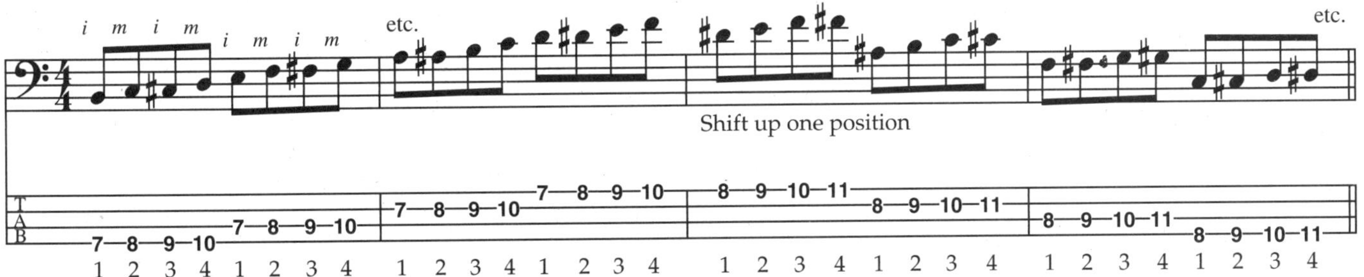

WHAT ASCENDS MUST DESCEND

Here's what the exercise looks like when you start on the 4th finger and come down. Start up high on the neck and work your way down one position at a time.

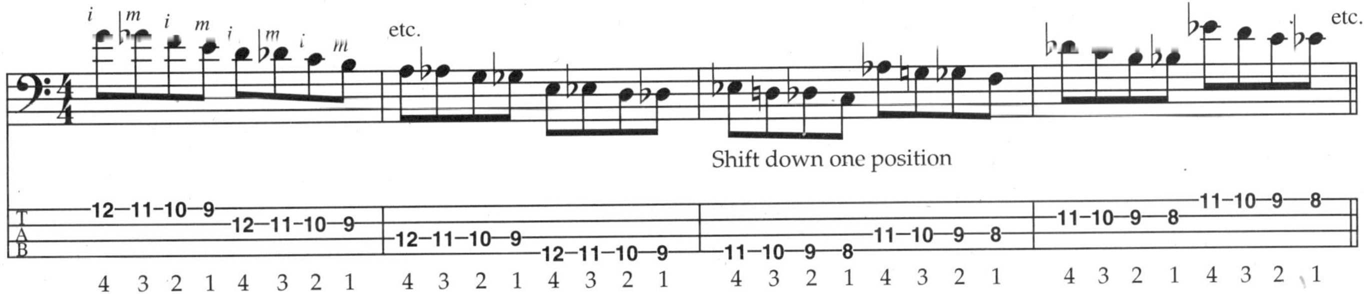

THE ON/OFF SWITCH: WORKING YOUR FLEXORS AND EXTENSORS

Here are some exercises to help you hone your flexor and extensor twitch responses. The goal here is to make notes with as little extraneous movement as possible, and to learn to operate each finger without all the other fingers going all "crazy dance team competition" on you. This is actually one big exercise that's split up into pieces so you can get the motions down.

WORKING THE 2ND FINGER FLEXOR AND EXTENSOR

For the first piece, you will hold the 1st finger down on the 7th fret while your 2nd finger frets and releases the note on the 8th fret. Keep in mind that you are working the twitch responses of the 2nd finger here, so concentrate only on the finger that's doing the work. Fretting works the flexor, releasing works the extensor. Try to be as robot-like as possible, as this is mechanical stuff.

WORKING THE 3RD AND 4TH FINGER FLEXORS AND EXTENSORS

The following exercises will work the 3rd and 4th finger. The 1st finger is already well developed in this area, so we're not going to give it a specific exercise.

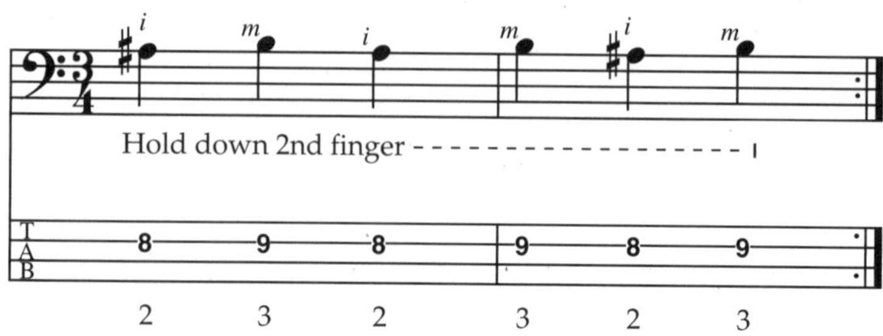

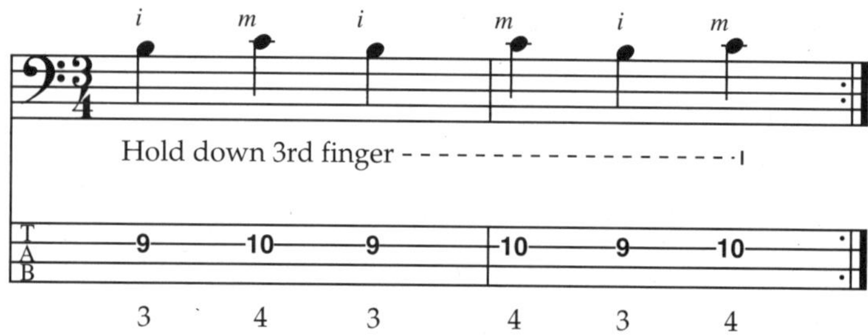

WE'LL BE BACK AFTER THIS WORD ABOUT TIME SIGNATURES

In this book, you'll see several different time signatures, which allow the meter to adapt to the needs of the exercise. Often, the time signature will have a 4 on the bottom, indicating that each quarter note is one beat. The time signature $\frac{4}{4}$ has four quarter notes per bar, $\frac{3}{4}$ has three quarter notes, and $\frac{6}{4}$ has six quarter notes.

If the time signature has an 8 on the bottom, the top number will be a multiple of 3 (as in $\frac{6}{8}$, $\frac{9}{8}$, $\frac{12}{8}$). These meters group the eighth notes into groups of three, like *triplets* (three notes in the time of two). Each "triplet" is felt as one pulse, or beat. For example, the $\frac{9}{8}$ example shown below is felt as three beats of eighth-note triplets. $\frac{6}{8}$ would be felt as two beats of triplets, and $\frac{12}{8}$ would be felt as four beats of triplets.

Here's the big exercise with all the components put together, working up the neck on the 2nd string. Try it on other strings as well. Remember to hold down the 1st finger while you're working the 2nd finger, and so on. This is not a speed exercise, so go slowly and concentrate on accuracy, economy, and synchronization.

Note that your picking will alternate throughout, so each new beat and each bar begin with a different picking finger. It may help to emphasize the beats by accenting them. To do this, play the first note of each triplet group a little louder than the others. (See accenting tip on page 23.)

The On/Off Machine Exercise Going Up the Neck

Here's what it looks like coming back down the neck.

The On/Off Machine Exercise Descending from the 12th Fret

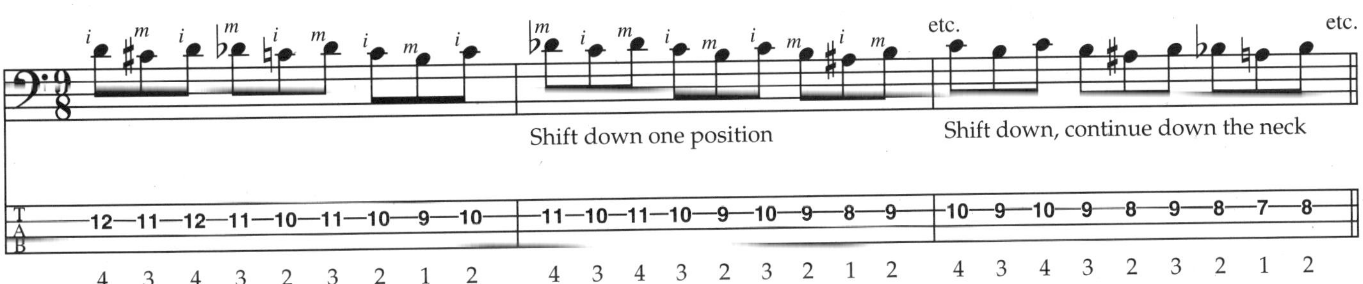

TONIGHT'S MIDNIGHT MOVIE: *THE MANY FINGERS OF DR. BASSISTO (OR, THERE'S MORE THAN ONE WAY TO BUST A GROOVE)*

It's time to take a little detour and talk about right-hand techniques. The electric bass was originally developed to be used equally by players of two radically different instruments, the upright bass and the guitar. As it grew in popularity, players invented, or adapted, many different ways to make sound on the strings with the picking hand. All of these techniques create unique sounds, and they're all worth trying out.

REST STROKES AND TWO-FINGER ALTERNATE PICKING

Most of the music in this book is shown using the two-finger method of playing. This method uses the index and middle finger of the picking hand (indicated by the letters *i* and *m*). You'll get the biggest and fullest sound possible if you use *rest strokes*. To play a rest stroke, use your *i* or *m* finger to play a note by pulling your finger tip across the string and following through with the motion until your finger comes to rest on the next lower-pitched string. When playing the lowest string, some players will use the thumb as a stopping point for the rest stroke.

One of the most popular methods of playing bass is to alternate the fingers (*i–m–i–m–i–m*), allowing more efficiency and speed than with one finger. This is the method shown in this book, but you can adapt nearly all of the exercises in this book to other styles of playing. Try to make the finger strokes as equal in tone and volume as possible.

HOW TO MAKE FINGERPICKING MORE ECONOMICAL

Economy fingerpicking is an adaptation of the basic alternating strokes that aid in crossing strings. When you are moving to a higher-pitched string, you alternate strokes as normal. When you move to an adjacent, lower-pitched string, you use the same finger to play the higher and lower string. This allows you to "drag" one finger across two strings, instead of changing fingers. Many bass players make this adjustment subconsciously.

Below is an example that shows standard alternate picking and the adjusted economy fingerpicking. Notice that as you move from string 1 back to string 2, the *m* finger plays twice in a row. The idea is that the rest stroke for string 1 has already landed the *m* finger on string 2, so it might as well do the job (since it's already there!). Some of the exercises in this book will be shown with alternate picking and some will be shown with economy fingerpicking. You can adapt these exercises to either style. If you change a picking pattern, it may help to write the new one in with a pencil so you remember it.

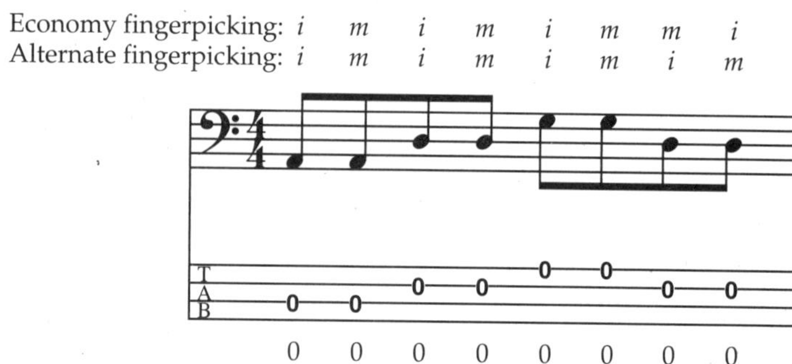

PLAYING WITH A PICK

Many rock, pop, and even jazz bassists play with a pick. Some pickstyle players alternate downstrokes and upstrokes just as they would alternate the *i* and *m* fingers. Other players adapt the picking to the needs of the moment, using a combination of downstrokes, upstrokes, and alternation to get the job done. As with alternating fingerstyle, the goal is to get the sound of the strokes as even in tone and volume as possible. Below is the exercise from the previous page shown with fingerpicking and with the symbols for playing with a pick. Notice that the pick strokes alternate with the count of the eighth notes—the numbered beats are downstrokes, while the "ands" (&s) are upstrokes.

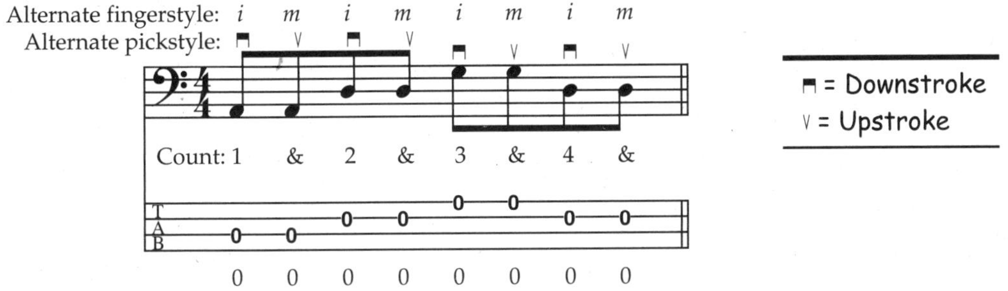

THUMBSTYLE

Some of the earliest players of the electric bass played all of the notes with the thumb of the picking hand, often using rest strokes that came to rest on the next higher string. This gives a deep sound that is still used by many players. The thumbstyle sacrifices some speed and definition for a deep, booming sound that mimics the sound of the upright bass.

SLAPPING AND POPPING

This is another unique style of playing based on using the thumb like a drumstick that strikes the string by bouncing it off of the fretboard (the slap), and popping a higher string by hooking the index or middle finger under the string and pulling up until the string pops off of the finger. Couch potato time is actually a great opportunity to work on slapping and popping, but keep in mind that it won't work for every situation or every exercise. For more on slapping and popping, check out pages 32–33.

WHILE WE'RE AT IT, WHAT IF YOUR BASS HAS MORE STRINGS?

The examples in this book are shown on the four-string electric bass. If you have more strings on your bass, just adapt the exercises to include your extra strings. Most of these exercises do not have to be tied to specific notes and keys. They are finger patterns meant to move around the neck so that your hand gets to experience lots of different positions on the fretboard.

THE ROGUE FINGER: ADDING STRING CROSSING TO THE MOTHER OF ALL MINDLESS FRETBOARD EXERCISES

This is a set of exercises based on the old 1-2-3-4 exercises you learned so long ago (page 14). The challenge here is to displace one finger in the pattern to the next string, so that your fingers get some practice crossing back and forth on adjacent strings. These are tricky at first, but they sound cool when you get them going. These exercises are shown with economy fingerpicking, which uses the same picking finger for two notes in a row when moving from a high string to a low string. Once these exercises can be easily played as written, practice them with eighth notes.

Be sure to practice your exercises with *legato* phrasing. The Italian musical term legato indicates that each note endures until the next note is sounded, so that the sound is not interrupted as you go from note to note. The opposite of legato is *staccato*, meaning the notes are played short and detached with a bit of silence between them.

Displacing Finger 2—Ascending

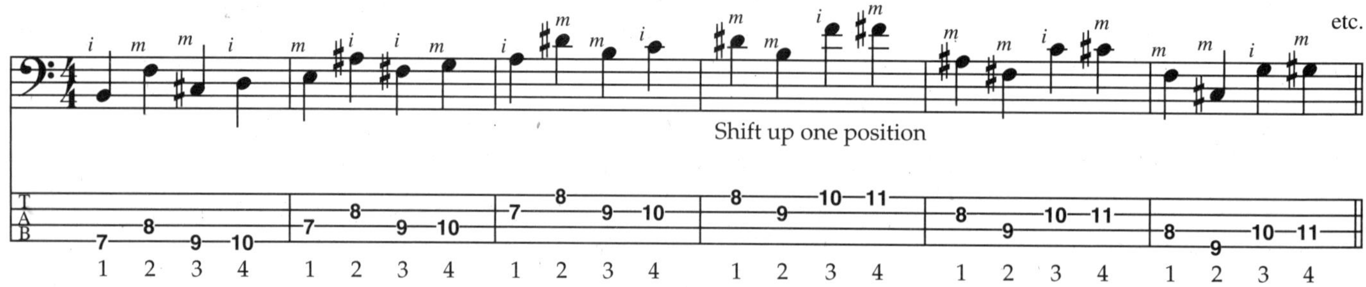

Displacing Finger 2—Descending

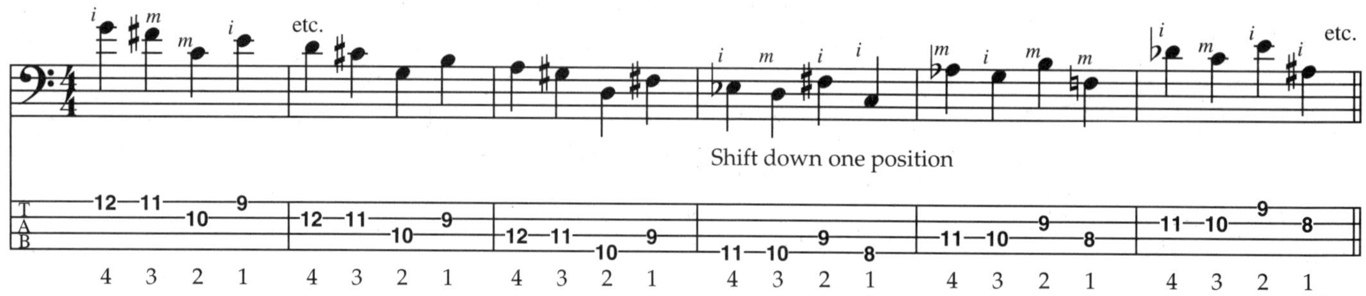

Displacing Finger 3—Ascending

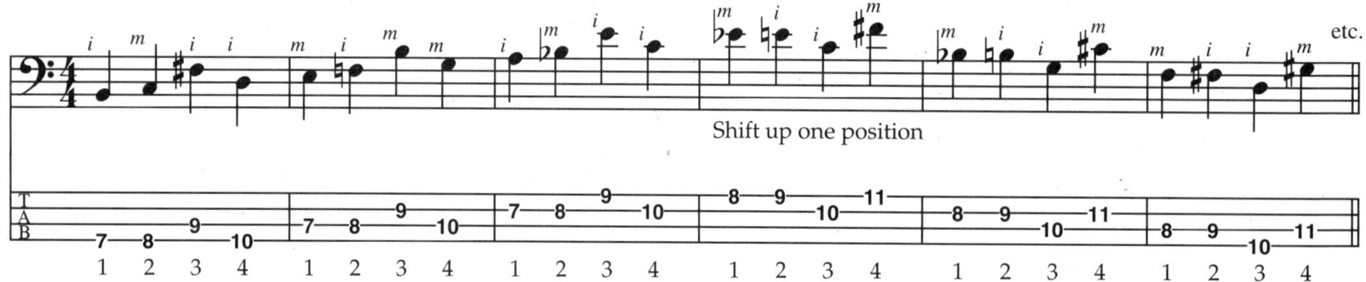

Displacing Finger 3—Descending

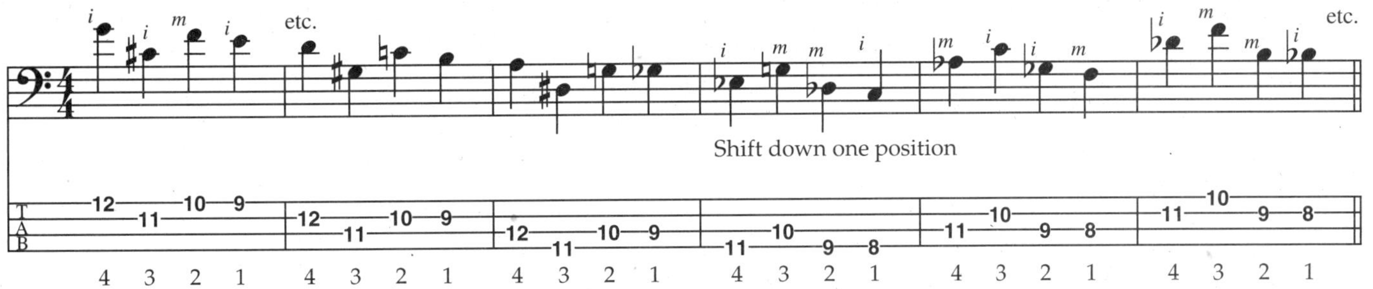

Displacing Finger 4—Ascending

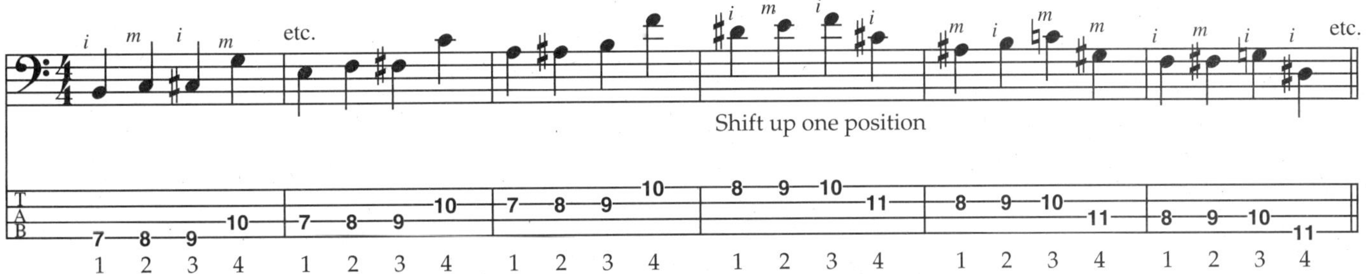

There are two approaches you could take to the 4th finger displacement while descending. Try them both.

Displacing Finger 4—Descending (Version 1)

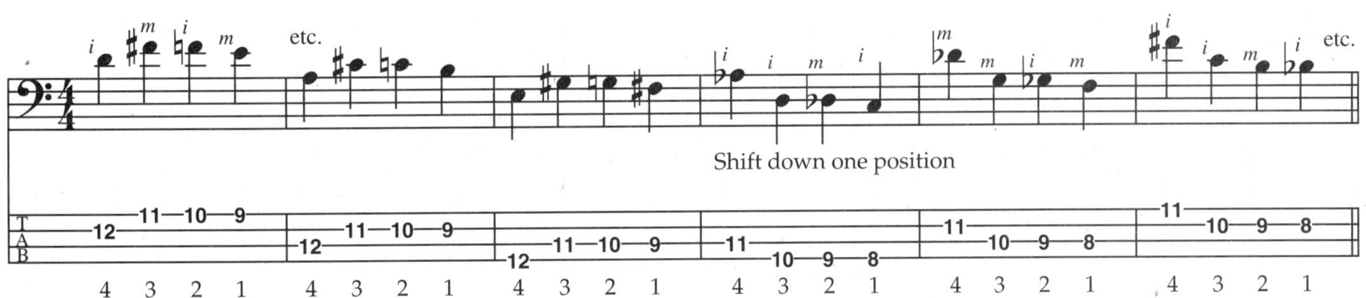

Displacing Finger 4—Descending (Version 2)

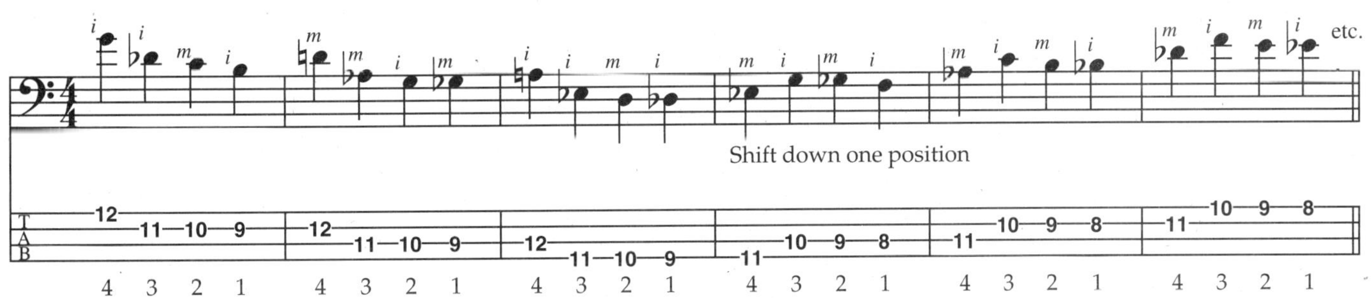

WORKING IN THREES

One of the best ways to develop your alternate picking agility is to practice three notes per string. The following exercises cover all of the three-finger combinations, ascending as you work from string 4 to string 1, then descending as you work back from string 1 to 4 (after a position shift). Economy fingerpicking is indicated in the example, but you could also try strict alternate picking instead.

Fingers 1-2-3

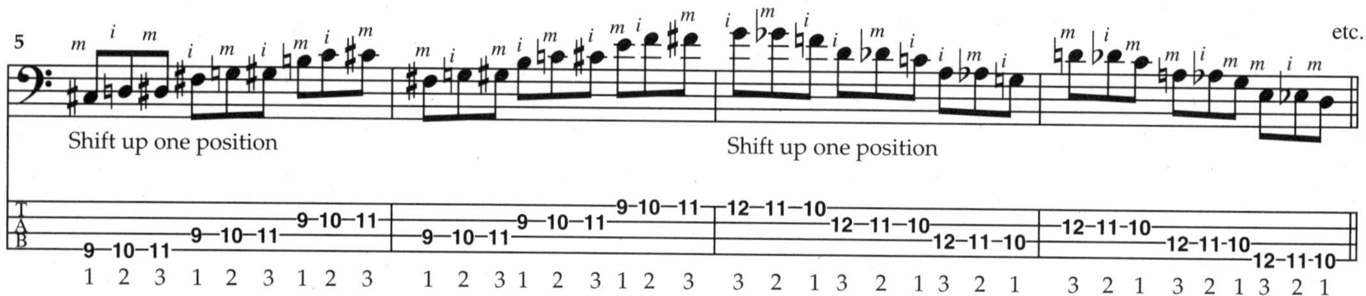

Fingers 1-2-4

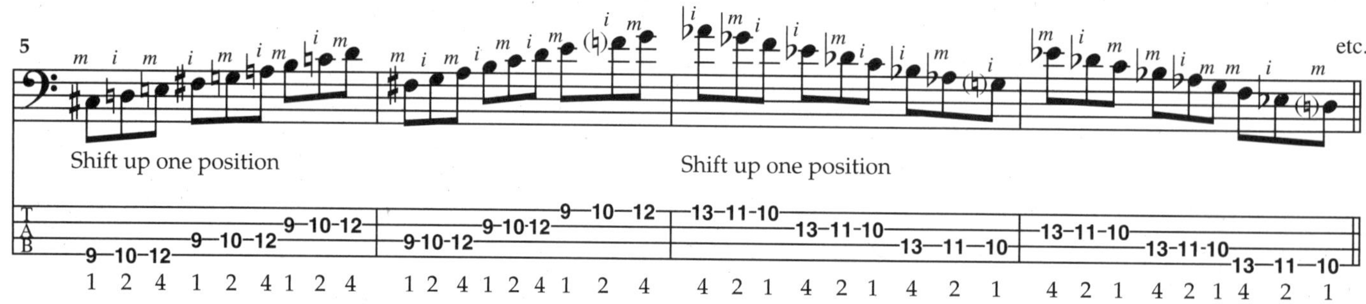

Fingers 1–3–4

> = Accent

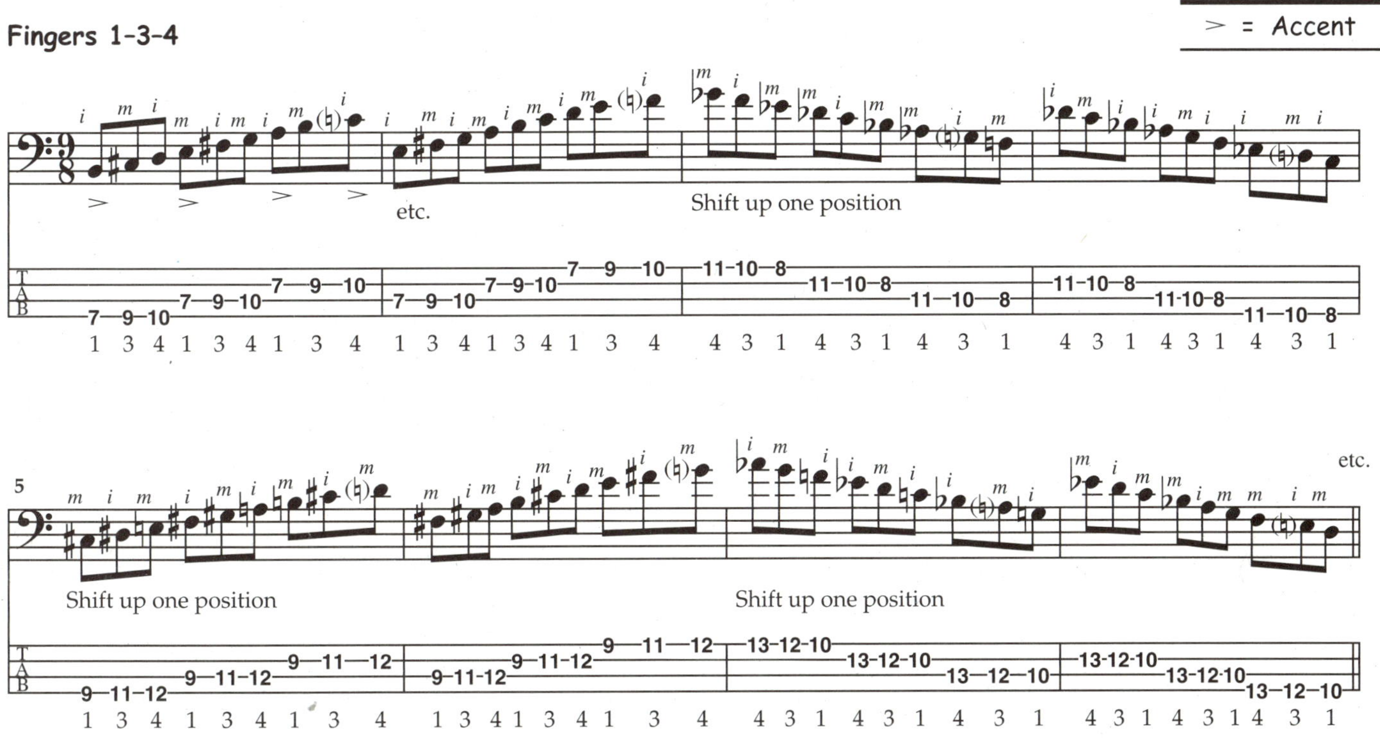

Fingers 2–3–4

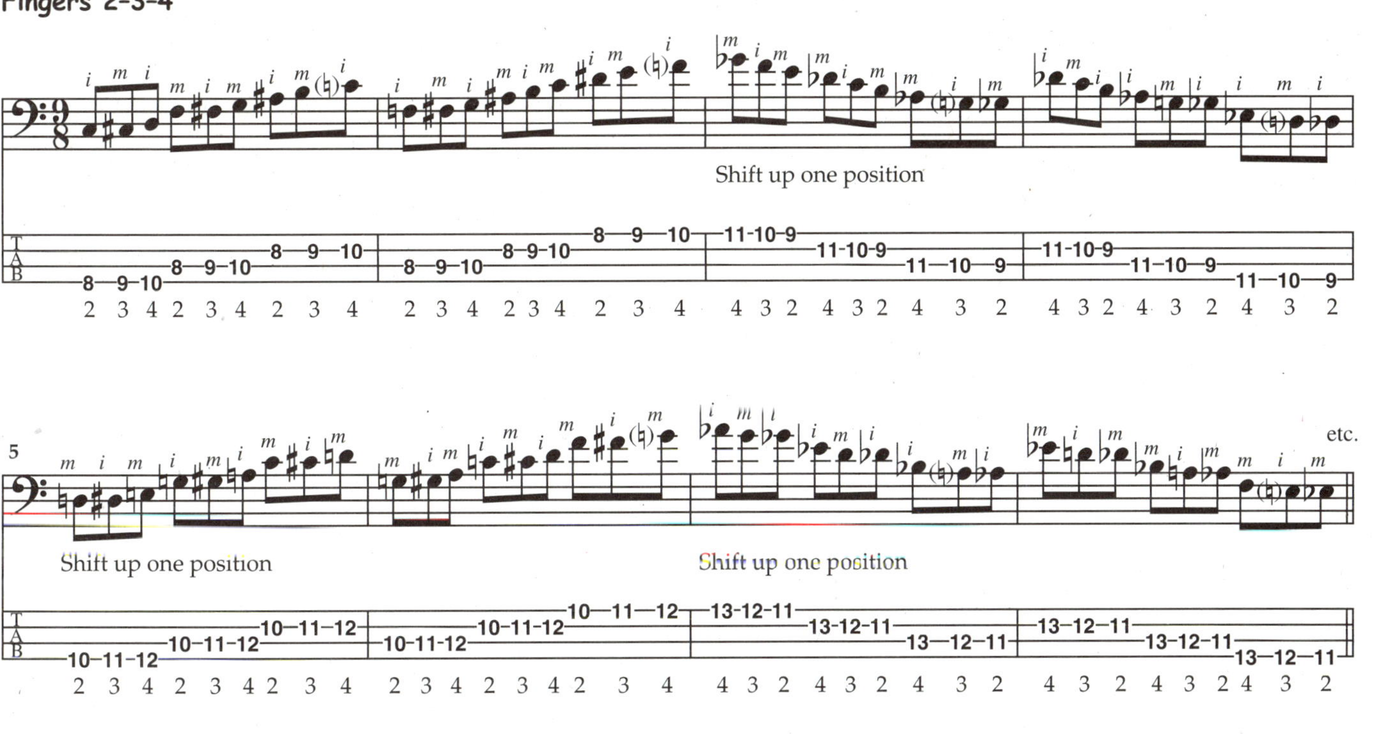

# HAMMER-ONS AND PULL-OFFS

You've been very picky so far. It's time to smooth things out with *slurs*. In music, a slur indicates that one note leads to the next without a distinct new articulation of the second note (such as a pick attack). On the bass, we make slurs by using *hammer-ons* and *pull-offs*. They are shown in music with an arc connecting two notes, and in TAB with an H for hammer-on and P for pull-off.

Here's an exercise to warm up your hammer-ons going up the neck.

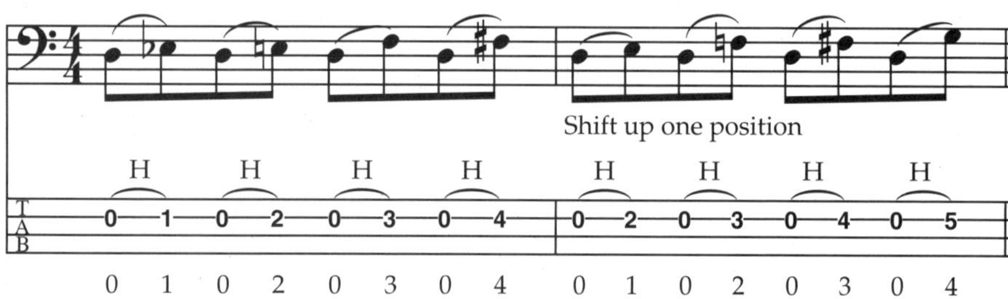

This one covers pull-offs.

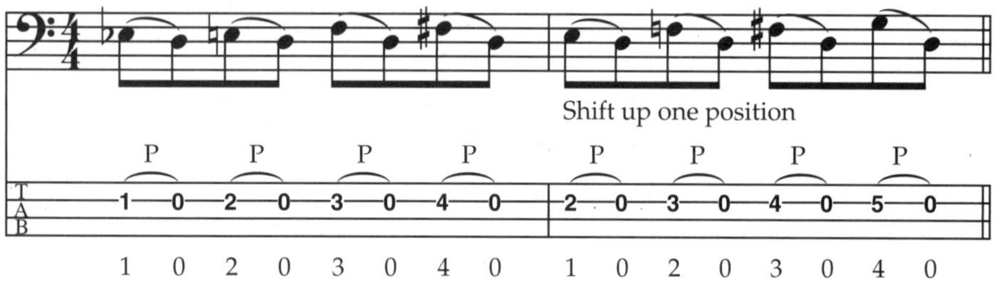

The next two exercises cover all the possible hammer-ons and pull-offs (except the 1st finger). The A exercise lets you repeat each move, then the B exercise condenses it all into one bar.

> ## TIPS FOR BETTER H'S AND P'S
>
> 1. A good hammer-on is all about follow-through. Imagine your finger is going to keep going all the way to the wood of the fingerboard.
>
> 2. A good pull-off requires the finger making the pull-off to snap off the string in a plucking motion. If you just lift straight up, you won't hear the slurred note. To execute a pull-off, you need to have both of the notes pressed down before you start.
>
> 3. Listen to the sound you make. If you can't hear each hammer-on or pull-off note loud and clear, go back and give it some more work.

Hammer-Ons

Pull-Offs

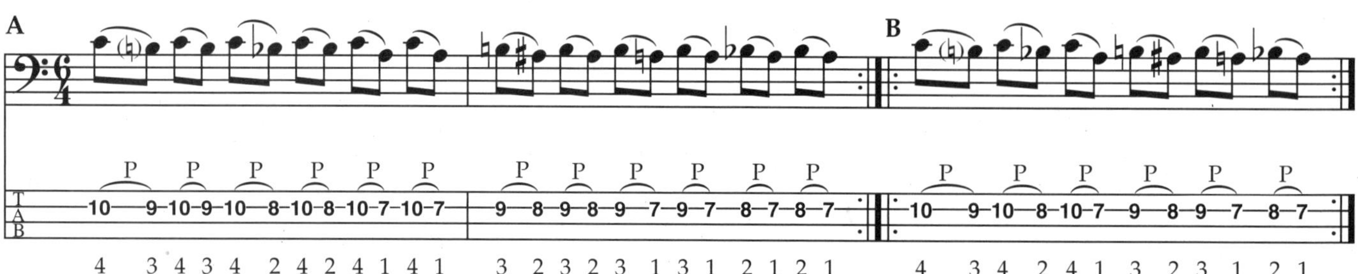

TAKE A TRILL RIDE

Here you'll be working out the skills you need to play longer slurred phrases and *trills* (fast alternations between two notes). Notice that you pick only once per bar. This should allow you almost enough time to reach for a potato chip before the next bar. Try this exercise on different strings and in different spots on the neck. Remember that you'll need to hold down the lower of the trilled notes for the whole bar. Make sure you can hear all the notes!

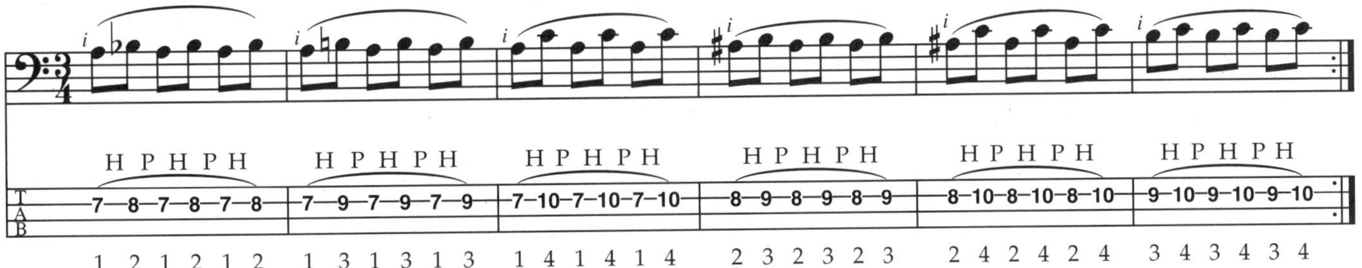

NOW IN TRIPLE STRENGTH FORMULA

The next exercise will help you work out in triplets. You'll pick the first note of the triplet, then hammer-on or pull-off the next two. Every three-finger combination is represented. The exercise is shown on the 2nd string at 7th position, but you should move it around to other strings and positions for variety. You may need to work on this exercise one bar at a time for a while.

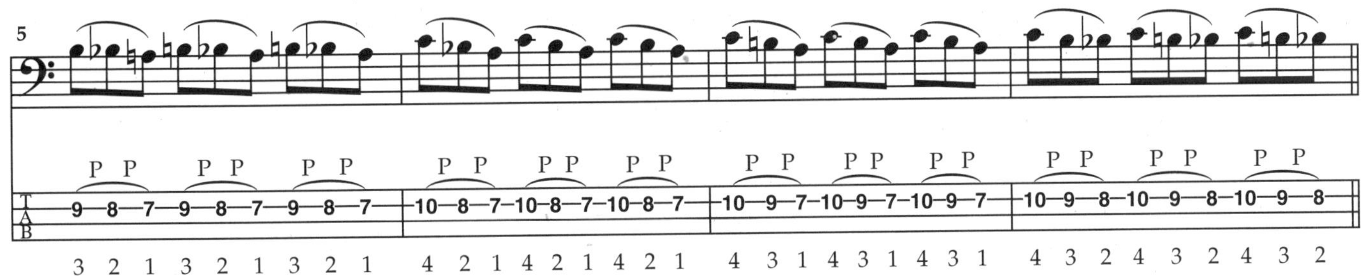

BASS SCALES (A FISHY SUBJECT)

There's not enough room in this book to teach you all about scales and how to use them. But, if you know a scale or two, here are some ideas on getting the most out of them during mindless couch potato practicing time. For the following exercises, you're going to use a C Major scale. You could adapt these exercises to any key or type of scale you wish; they're just patterns.

Below is a C Major scale. The major scale is made by starting on the *key note* (the note the scale is named after, in this case C) and following this pattern of whole steps and half steps: whole–whole–half–whole–whole–whole–half. This C Major scale begins with finger 2 on string 4 at the 8th fret, which places it in 7th position.

C Major Scale (7th Position, Starting on Finger 2)

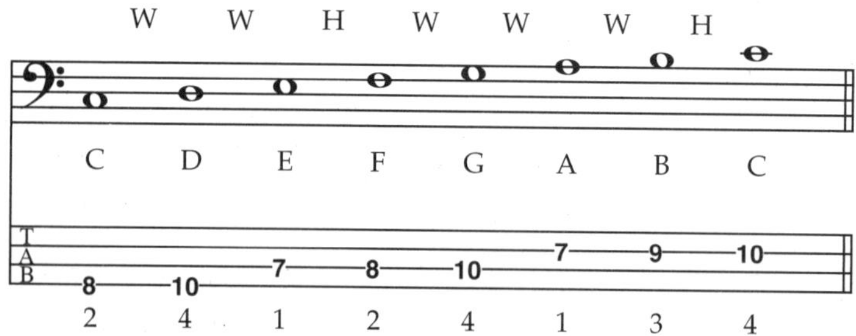

And now, let's play a bunch of patterns. In the first one, follow this pattern: skip up a *3rd* (every other scale tone is an *interval,* or distance, of a 3rd), go down a scale tone, skip up a 3rd, go down a scale tone, etc. For simplicity, this is shown with alternate fingerpicking.

Ascending: Up a 3rd, Down a Scale Tone

Here's the descending version of the pattern.

Descending: Down a 3rd, Up a Scale Tone

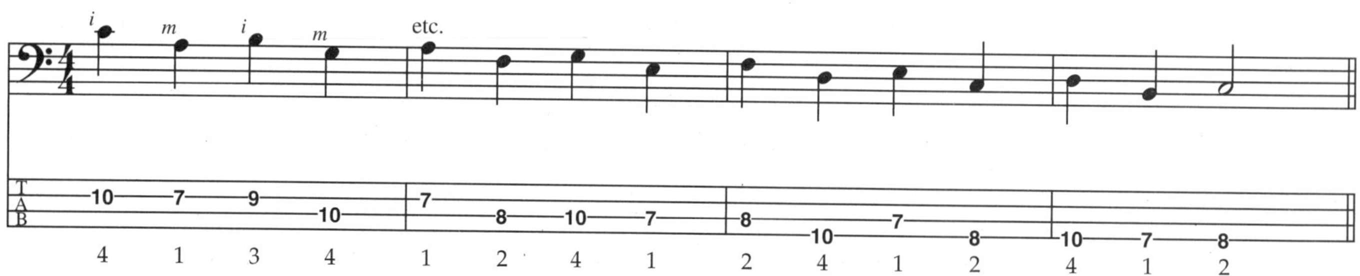

These patterns are called *sequences*. A sequence is a short pattern of notes that is duplicated starting on the next scale tone up (or down). Sequences are used heavily in classical music (composer J. S. Bach was a big fan of them during the Baroque era). They are also used in shredding solos to help get maximum notage out of a small set of notes. If you are using a pattern and then "rubber stamping" it up the scale, you don't run out of notes as fast. In the first two bars, the brackets in the TAB will help you see the initial pattern; the bars that follow show the sequences moving up the scale. The following examples are shown using economy fingerpicking. Adjust the picking to your needs.

Sequence: Up Two Consecutive Scale Tones, Down a 3rd

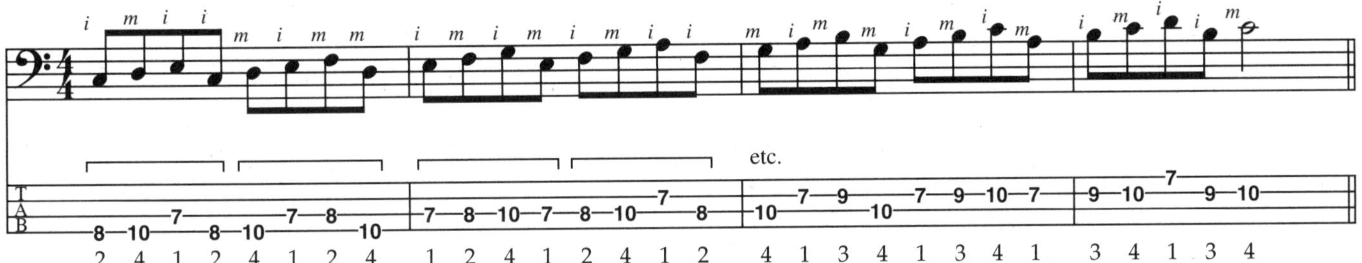

These examples are written in eighth notes, but that doesn't mean they have to be fast. Here's another pattern. Once you've got it, just reverse the pattern to come down from the top note.

Sequence: Up Three Consecutive Scale Tones, Down a 3rd

This one's in triplets to challenge your picking. It helps to accent the first note of each triplet so you can feel the three notes per beat. It's shown ascending and descending.

Triplet Sequence: Up Two Consecutive Scale Tones, Down One Scale Tone

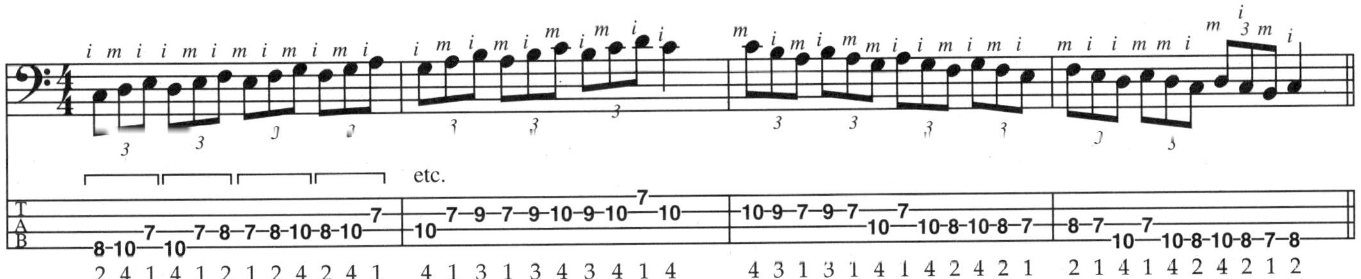

AN ARPEGGIO IS NOT A STRING OF ISLANDS

That would be an "archipelago," which you would know if you watched the science channel instead of those reality shows you love so much. An *arpeggio* is a chord that has been broken up so each note is played separately. Arpeggio exercises are great to work on for your understanding of chords and your knowledge of the fretboard.

To play arpeggios that include all the notes of a chord in order, you need to know something about how chords are constructed.

MAJOR TRIAD

To the right is a C Major *triad* (a three-note chord). It contains a root (C), a 3rd (E), and a 5th (G), which correspond to the 1st, 3rd, and 5th notes of a C Major scale.

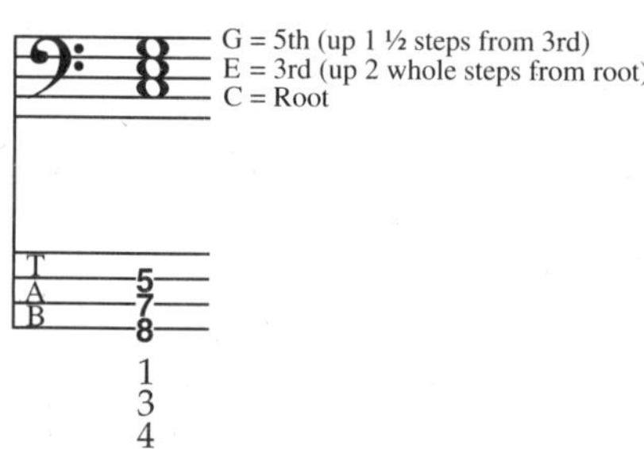

MINOR TRIAD

To the right is a C Minor triad. To make a minor triad, you lower the 3rd of a major triad by one half step (which is then referred to as the ♭3rd, or "flat 3rd").

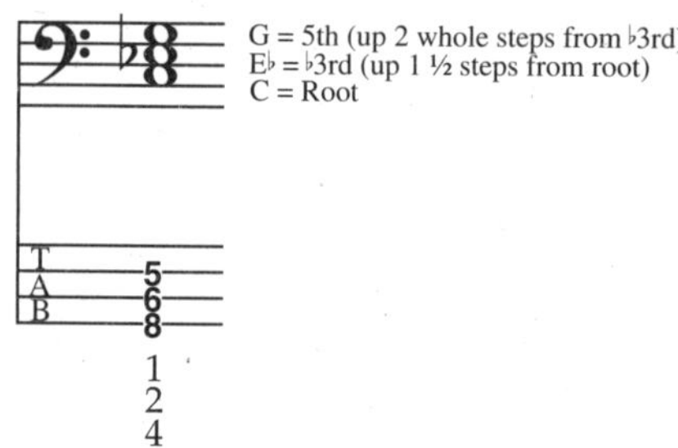

The following exercises will help you work with arpeggios that include the roots, 3rds, and 5ths of the triads. These arpeggios can help you learn the fretboard by showing you an outline of all the chord tones for a particular chord. On the bass, there are many ways to finger a given arpeggio. Once you learn some basic fingerings, you can move them around the neck to find other chords.

The most compact fingering for a major chord arpeggio begins on finger 2. Below, we have some arpeggio exercises for a C Major chord starting with finger 2 on the 8th fret of the 4th string. Exercise A is just the root, 3rd and 5th. Exercise B includes the octave of the root, so an adjustment to the fingering helps make this smoother. Exercise C shows two octaves of the arpeggio, which is aided by a position shift and fingering adjustment as you transition to the second octave.

C Major Arpeggios Starting on Finger 2

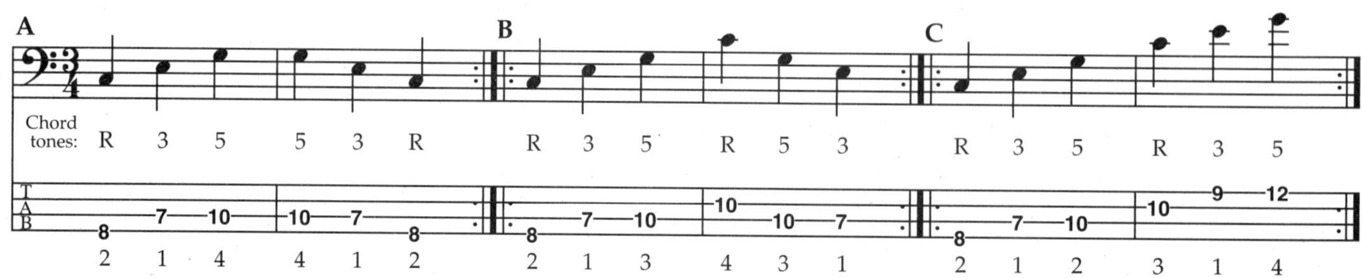

If you lower the 3rds of the major arpeggio by one half step, they become minor 3rds ($\flat$3).
Right away you have a problem. If you started on finger 2, you'd have a stretch to get the next
chord tone. The minor arpeggio works better starting on finger 3, with the $\flat$3 played by the 1st
finger, then stretching or shifting the hand up to get the 5th of the chord with the 4th finger.
Notice the adjusted fingerings in the B and C exercises to help the notes flow better.

C Minor Arpeggios Starting on Finger 3

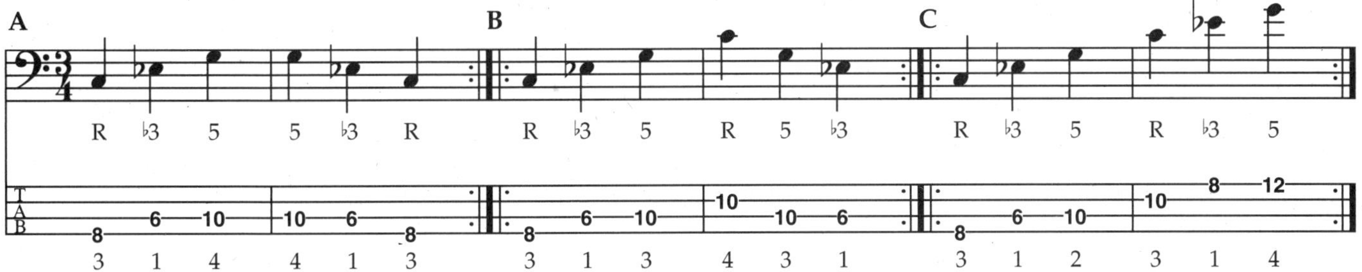

Practice the major and minor arpeggios in different spots on the neck using different chords.
These arpeggios can be very useful in building bass lines that carry more information about the
chord progression than just the root of the chord. There's no reason to be one of those bass
players that doesn't care if the chord is major or minor.

DIATONIC TRIADS

Many chord progressions can be built simply by using the notes in the major scale. Below is a C
Major scale that has been harmonized into triads. The first beat of every bar is a step in the
scale, which is then used as the root of a triad. If you use only the notes from the scale to form
the triads, you get the *diatonic* triads, which means the triads "belonging to the scale, or key."
Diatonic triads built from a major scale follow this order: major–minor–minor–major–major–
minor–diminished.

The chords are labeled with Roman numerals corresponding to the scale
degree on which the chord is built. Upper case numerals denote major
triads, lower case denote minor, and a lower case numeral with a superscript
circle (○) is *diminished*. Don't let that diminished triad on the 7th degree
scare you! A diminished triad has a minor 3rd ($\flat$3) and a diminished 5th ($\flat$5).
Play a minor triad, lower the 5th by one half step and you'll be just fine.

Following is the whole series of diatonic triads using the fingerings you've
been practicing. Once you've got it, try it in every key and on different
strings.

Roman Numeral Review	
I or i 1	V or v 5
II or ii 2	VI or vi 6
III or iii 3	VII or vii 7
IV or iv 4	

C Major Diatonic Chord Arpeggios Starting on Fingers 2 and 3

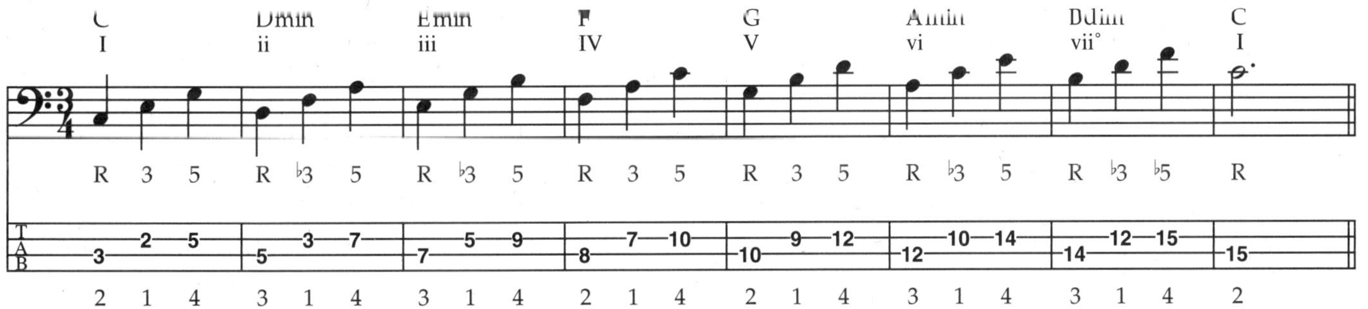

MORE ARPEGGIO FINGERINGS AND DIATONIC TRIADS

Here's a new fingering for your triads, starting on finger 4. You'll need three strings to cover
each triad, so don't start any higher than the 3rd string. If you're strong and can stretch your
fingers, you can use these fingerings to play all three notes of the triad like a guitar chord.
Watch for the fingering adjustment in the high octave of exercise C, it changes to the old
finger 2 start note.

C Major Arpeggios Starting on Finger 4

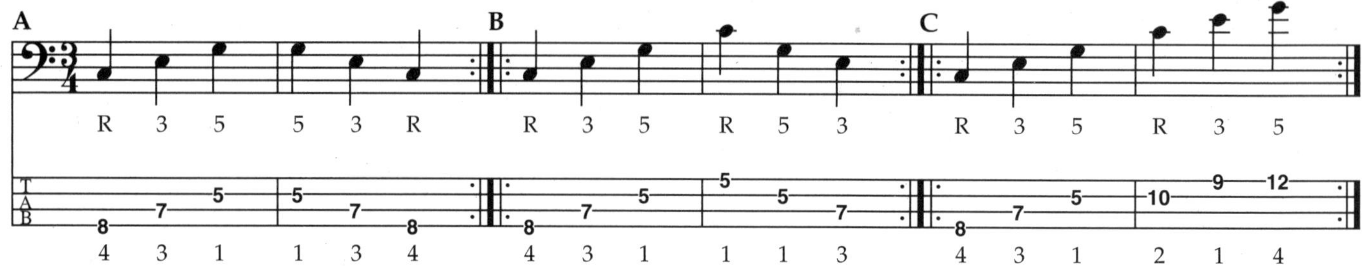

Now, let's look at the minor fingerings.

C Minor Arpeggios Starting on Finger 4

Following are the diatonic triads for the key of C Major. Since the fingerings require a four-
fret spread, start on string 4 for the first few chords, then finish the scale with the roots
going up string 3.

C Major Diatonic Chord Arpeggios Starting on Finger 4

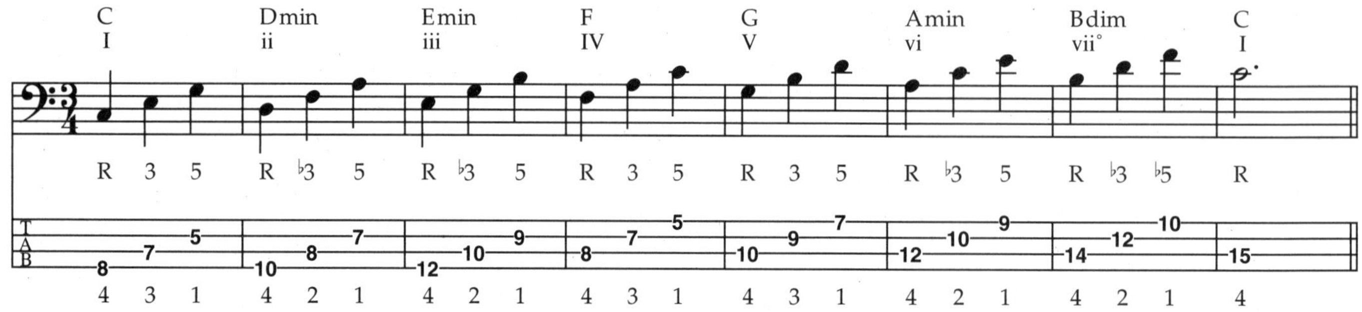

The final set of fingerings starts on the 1st finger. To play a major triad, you either have to stretch two whole steps up from the root to the 3rd, or you can shift your hand up into a new position. These exercises are fingered so that you begin on the root with your 1st finger, then shift two frets up so that the 3rd finger reaches the 3rd of the chord. Then, the 1st finger will be in position for the 5th of the chord on the next string. Many bass lines take advantage of this shift by sliding up to the 3rd of the chord from a fret or two below.

C Major Arpeggios Starting on Finger 1

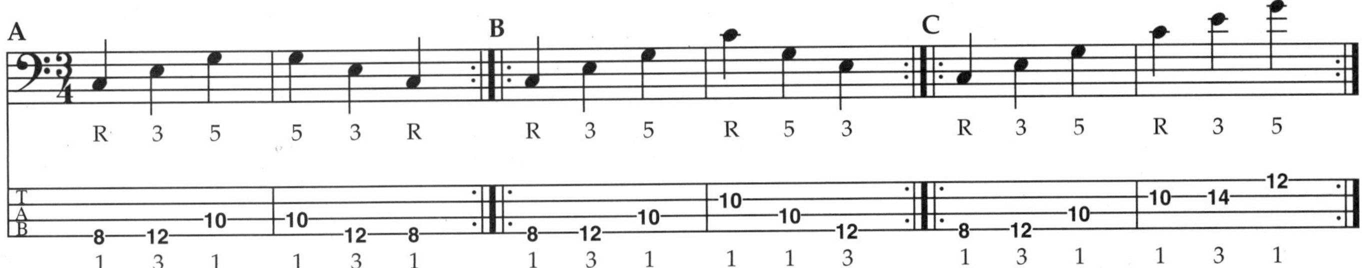

Below are the minor fingerings. These don't require a position shift, so you can use your 4th finger to play the ♭3 and your 3rd finger to play the 5th of the triad.

C Minor Arpeggios Starting on Finger 1

Now, let's look at the full progression of diatonic triads. It begins at the 3rd fret of the 3rd string so you can follow the whole scale up the 3rd string. You could also move some of the triads to other strings. Be sure to try these in other keys and in different orders so you can use them to make all kinds of music.

C Major Diatonic Chord Arpeggios Starting on Finger 1

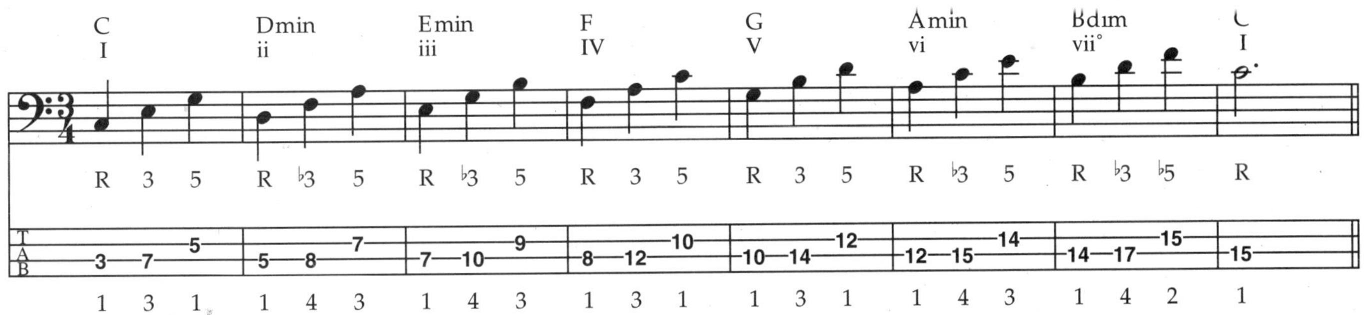

SLAPPING AND POPPING: WHEN IT ABSOLUTELY, POSITIVELY HAS TO BE FUNKY

On the next episode of "Afternoon Chat"—Is it possible to lead a fulfilling, bass-playing life without slapping and popping? Of course it is. If you are one of those people that think *slapping* and *popping* leads to the ruination of a perfectly good bass line, keep moving, nothing to see here. If you gotta have that funk, read on.

Slapping and popping is that special sound you hear in funk, rock, and even jazz bass playing that turns your bass strings into drums and your picking hand into a drumstick. It's all about rhythm and texture.

DO THE SLAP

1. To do the slap, first stick out your picking-hand thumb like a hitchhiker, or like The Fonz on *Happy Days*. (If you've never heard of either of these things, look them up on the Internet.)

2. Next, practice waggling your hand back and forth by rotating your forearm at the elbow. Let your thumb stay loose. This is the motion you will use for slapping.

3. Move your hand down to the strings of the bass, near the end of the fretboard. Using the waggling motion, bounce your thumb on the E string so the string slaps against the fretboard and the note sounds loud and clear. You have to stay loose and bouncy or the note won't come out and you'll bruise your thumb. Some players allow the thumb to rest on the next string on follow-through, which combines the idea of the slap with the idea of the rest stroke (see page 18).

DO THE POP

1. While holding your thumb out in the way-cool slapping position, curl your index or middle finger around into a hook shape. Upon slapping a note on the E string, allow the hooked finger to catch on the D string, hooking it from underneath. This is the position that starts the pop.

2. Using the hooked finger, pull your hand up and away from the bass, taking the string with you. You won't be able to go far, as the string will slip off of your finger and bounce back on the frets with a loud "thwap." That's the pop. You want that. You'll usually be popping fretted notes, which will allow you to immediately *damp* (mute) the popped note by relaxing your fretting finger.

Following are some slaps and pops using two A notes an octave apart. Slaps are indicated with an S and an accent. Pops are shown with a P, as well as a *staccato* marking (a dot centered on the notehead) that indicates the note should be cut short by relaxing the fretting finger.

$\underset{>}{S}$ = Slap

$\underset{\cdot}{P}$ = Pop

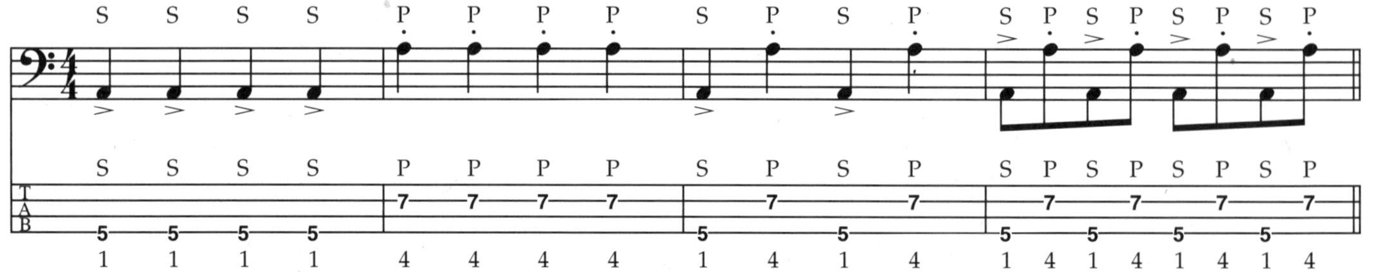

YOUR FRIEND THE OCTAVE

Octaves are the best place to start slapping and popping. You can move them around just by moving the same shape (like the notes in the previous exercise). Slapping and popping octaves doesn't interrupt the harmonic function of the bass line because both the slapped and popped notes are the same pitch.

GHOST NOTES

Ghost notes are damped, unpitched notes that are played to add a percussive element to the groove. You can incorporate them into your slapping and popping by muting notes with your fretting hand (usually by relaxing your finger pressure while staying on the string). Let's check out an example that shows ghost notes (marked with an × on the notehead) on the slap and on the pop. Your right hand will make the slap and pop motions the same way with dead notes as with normal notes. It's up to your left hand to do the muting.

× = Ghost note

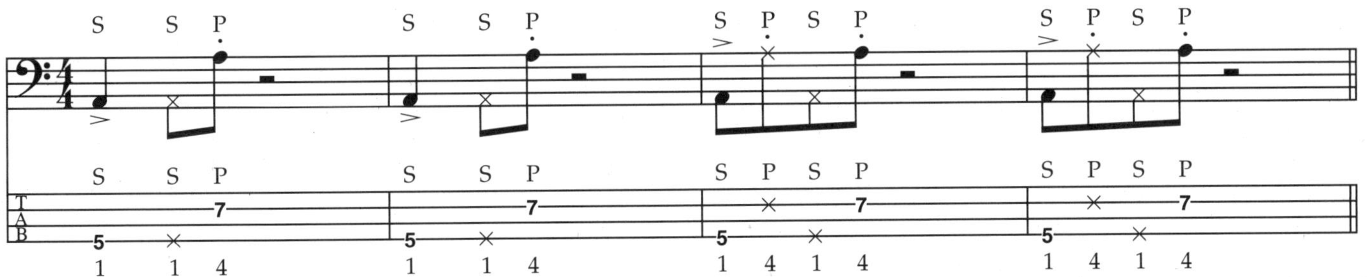

SLAP-HAMMER-DEADSLAP-POP

Here's a pattern to get you started on the way to world funk domination. Slap a note held by the 1st finger, 3rd string, hammer-on the 3rd finger, then mute that note and slap it again (this is the *dead-slap*, or *ghost-note slap*), then pop on the 4th finger, 1st string. After you get this down, move up a whole step and try it again. The B version adds a reversed "pop-slap" figure where the rests were in the A version.

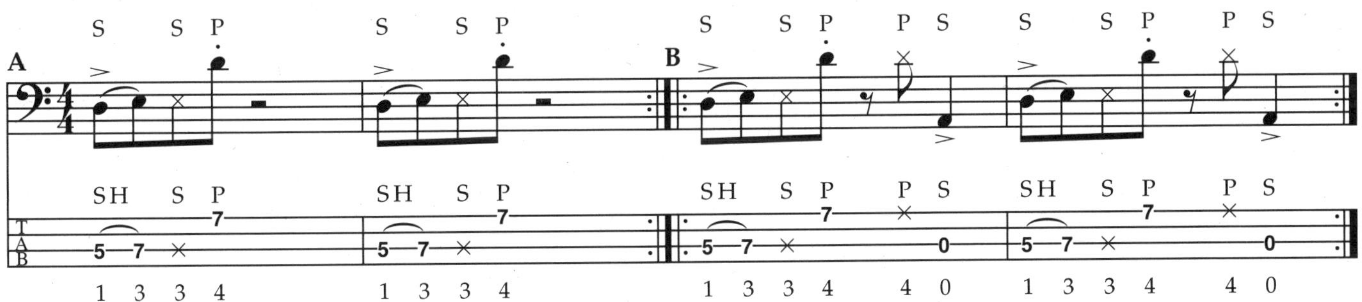

GET UP AND MOW THE LAWN! JUST KIDDING, MORE MINDLESS FINGER-TWISTERS

The next example is a challenging one. Take the "Mother of All Mindless Fretboard Exercises" and replace a note on each string with a rest. First you'll rest on the 2nd note on string 4, then the 3rd note on string 3, the 4th note on string 2, the 1st note on string 1, etc. Confused?

Once you've made it up to the top, shift up one fret and start descending using the same idea. The right-hand fingering is shown using strict alternation of *i* and *m* such that *i* is always playing downbeats (1, 2, 3, 4) and *m* is always playing "ands." You can alter the right-hand fingering to suit your playing style. Just keep in mind that on the bass, rests are cleaner if they are made by damping the string with a picking finger. Sometimes a rest made by relaxing the fretting finger will cause the lifting string to rattle against the fret.

The Wandering Rest

This example below works on your stretch between the 1st and 4th fingers. Depending on where you are on the neck, you may need to shift your hand a bit as well, but try to keep the notes as legato as possible. "The Inchworm" gets very difficult as you get down to the lower frets, so take it easy and don't hurt yourself!

The Inchworm

*Shift position

THE CHROMATIC SCALE, BECAUSE YOU NEVER KNOW WHEN YOU'RE GOING TO NEED ALL 12 NOTES

In this topsy-turvy world, it's good to know you can play all 12 half steps in a row if you want to. Following are some exercises for practicing the *chromatic scale,* which consists of all 12 half steps within an octave. There are two fingerings shown here. The first fingering uses four notes per string and requires a position shift every four notes. You'll also shift up one extra fret to begin your descent (just for fun). These chromatic scale fingerings can be started on any string at any fret, just follow the finger (and shifting) patterns to play them chromatically.

Chromatic Scale—Four Notes per String

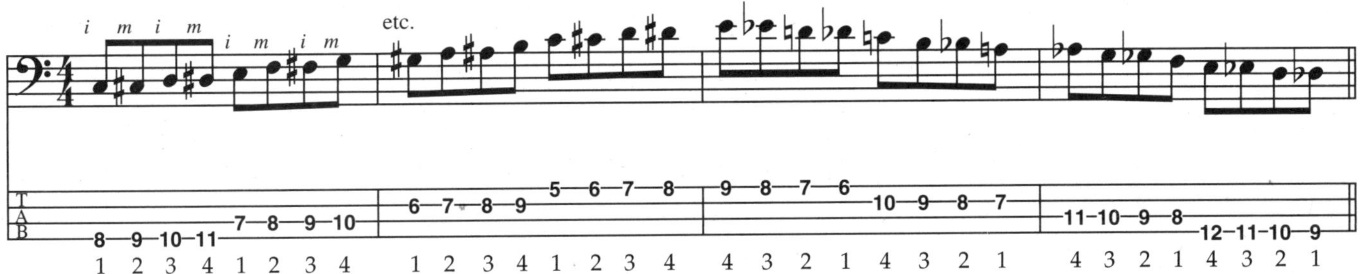

The second fingering uses five notes per string. You either play two notes with the 4th finger (shown ascending), or two notes with the 1st finger (shown descending).

Chromatic Scale—Five Notes per String

*Shift up one extra fret to begin descent

This space intentionally left blank
(so you can jot down the number of the pizza delivery place)

THE GREATEST BASS SCALES EVER: THE MAJOR AND MINOR PENTATONIC SCALES

At the risk of slightly overselling, these two scales are awfully helpful in improvising, learning more complex scales, and linking chord arpeggios and scales together. There are many ways to finger a pentatonic scale, but this section will focus on the sliding fingering that alternates between two notes and three notes per string. By getting these fingerings into both your mind and your muscle memory, you'll be well on your way to whizzing up and down the neck like a motocross racer.

MAJOR PENTATONIC SCALE

First up is the *major pentatonic scale,* which is like a major scale that is missing the 4th and 7th notes. Its formula is: 1–2–3–5–6. When you play the scale, it may sound familiar—the opening guitar riff to The Temptations' song "My Girl" is a major pentatonic scale. (Make sure you also check out bassist James Jamerson's great playing on that song!)

PUBLIC SERVICE ANNOUNCEMENT

For notes positioned two frets up from the 1st finger, we use either the 3rd finger or the 4th finger (which offers less of a stretch than the 3rd). There are good arguments for both options in different situations, so both are used in this book. If the finger shown isn't working for you, try the other one. It'll be our little secret.

And now, a word about slides...

SL = *Shift slide.* Play the first note, then slide up or down to a second note on the same string and pluck that note, too.

SL = *Legato slide.* Play the first note, then slide up or down to a second note on the same string. Only the first note is plucked.

And we're back. Here's a one-octave fingering in the key of A. This fingering/fretboard pattern is the basis for the rest of this section. The scale degrees are labeled.

Major Pentatonic Scale in A, Root on String 4

The following fingering is one octave higher. Notice that it repeats the same fretboard pattern, but you have to shift up at the end to get the last note.

Major Pentatonic Scale in A, Root on String 2

There are a couple of approaches you could take to stringing the one-octave patterns together.
The easiest is to repeat the pattern from the 1st finger when you reach the octave of the root.
You'll still have to shift up and grab the high A with your 4th finger.

Major Pentatonic Scale in A, Two Octaves (Option 1)

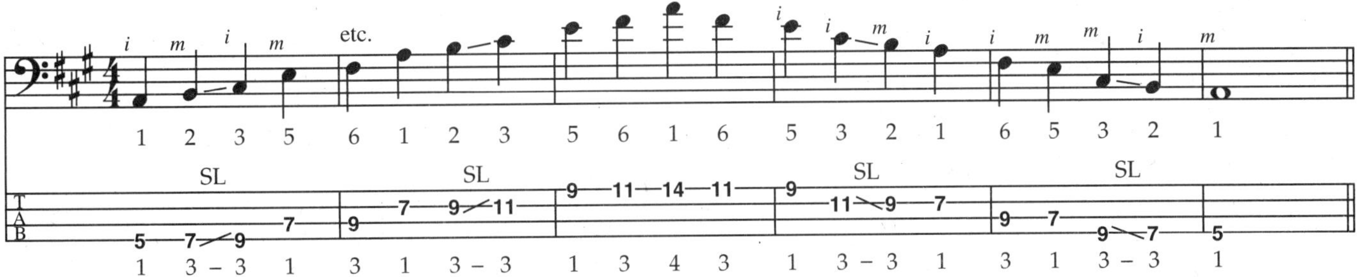

Another option is to play the first five notes, then shift up to a new octave on the same string.
This option has bigger leaps, but allows you to get further up the neck. If you start on a low
enough key (like F or G) and have enough frets, you can squeeze three octaves out of this
fingering.

Major Pentatonic Scale in A, Two Octaves (Option 2)

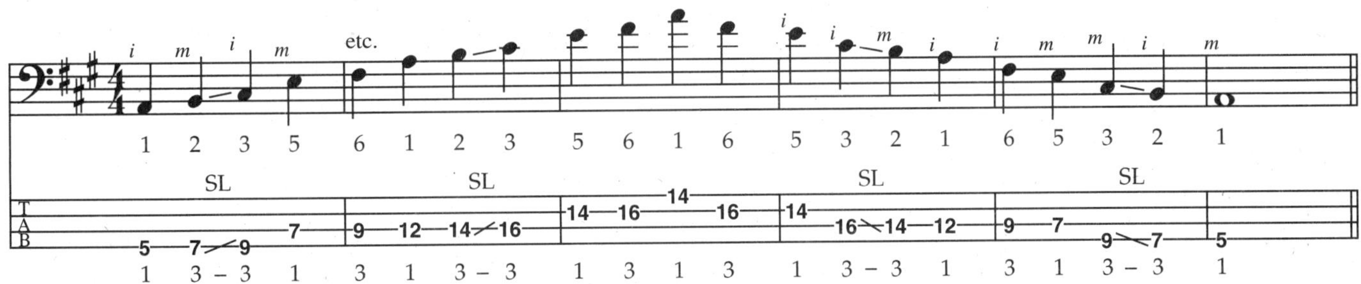

Use some of your couch potato time to teach your fingers these scales, and try different keys
and positions. Don't forget to experiment with improvisation using the scales. You can also use
the major pentatonic scale to make bass lines that can be moved from chord to chord. Here's a
progression that covers A, D, and G chords.

Major Pentatonic Chord Progression (Old School R&B Groove)

MINOR PENTATONIC SCALE

In the previous episode, you learned the major pentatonic sliding fingerings. Now, due to a cruel and not-very-unexpected plot twist, you must learn the *minor pentatonic* sliding fingerings.

The minor pentatonic scale contains the following scale degrees: 1-♭3-4-5-♭7. If you're really paying attention, you may have noticed the major pentatonic is like a major triad arpeggio with a couple of new notes added. Likewise, the minor pentatonic is like a minor triad arpeggio with notes 4 and ♭7 added.

The fingering is actually the same fretboard pattern as the major pentatonic, but starts at a different point in the sequence of notes. It may help to think of the minor pentatonic as starting on finger 3, while the major pentatonic starts on finger 1.

Minor Pentatonic Scale in A, Root on String 4

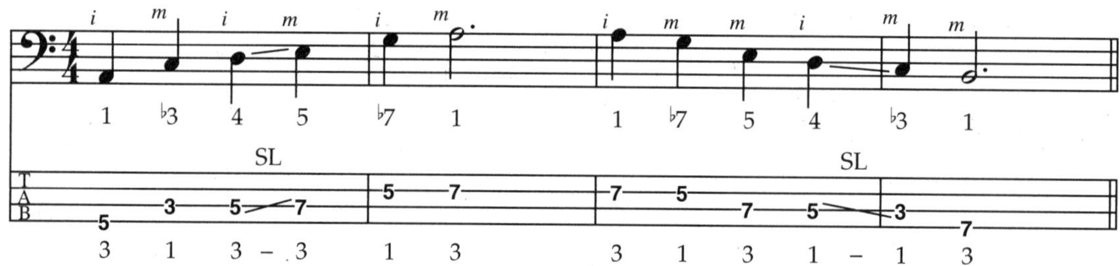

The next fingering, which starts on the 3rd string, is one octave higher than the previous one.

Minor Pentatonic Scale in A, Root on String 3

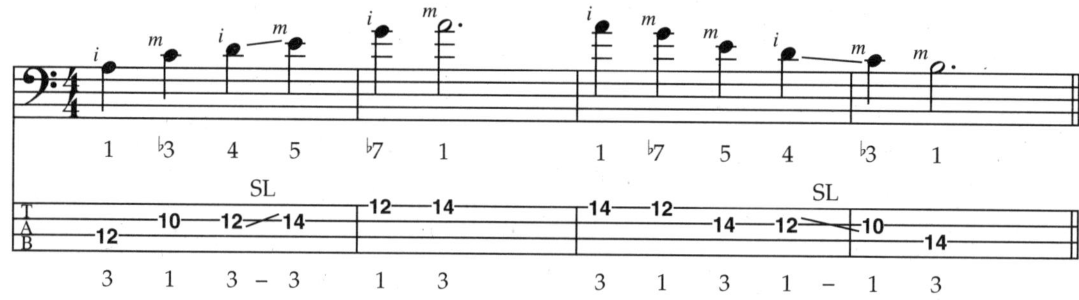

As with the major pentatonic, there are a couple of ways to make a two-octave fingering for the minor pentatonic scale. If you play the first octave fingering and then begin the next octave where you left off, you'll have to finish the scale by shifting up the 1st string in the following manner.

Minor Pentatonic Scale in A, Two Octaves (Option 1)

Another option is to play the first four notes, then shift up into the next octave on the $\flat$7 note to finish the scale in the higher octave.

Minor Pentatonic Scale in A, Two Octaves (Option 2)

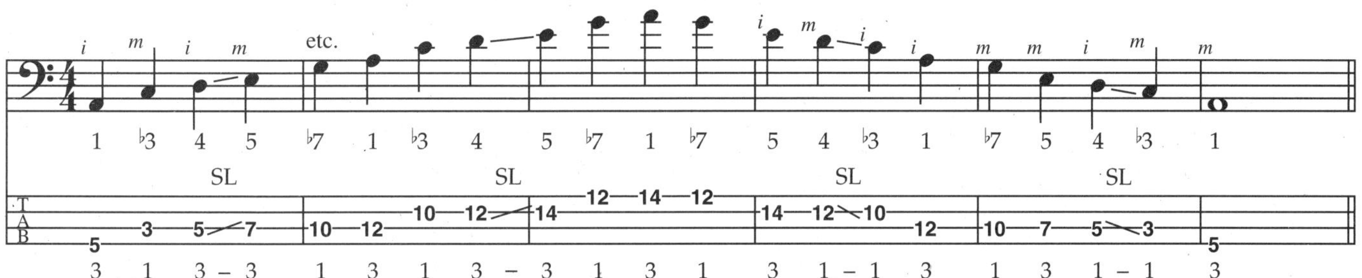

As with the major pentatonic scale, you can use the minor pentatonic to create riffs and move them to different chords. Thanks to the magic of the blues (and its ability to blend major and minor sounds), minor pentatonic riffs can even be played against major or dominant 7th chords. Here's a groove that uses an A Minor Pentatonic scale over an A7 chord and a D Minor Pentatonic scale over a D7 chord.

Minor Pentatonic Funky Blues Groove in A

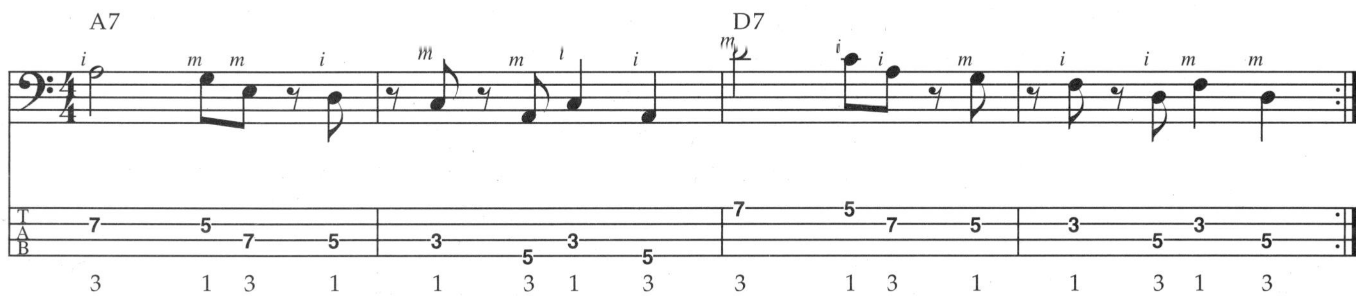

AUTO-PILOT BASS LINES: PATTERNS YOU SHOULD BE ABLE TO PLAY IN YOUR SLEEP

One of the best uses of repetitive practice time is building an arsenal of those classic bass line finger patterns that can be used with many chords in many styles. The next few pages are devoted to patterns that build on the skills you've picked up in the rest of this book. The picking indications will generally follow economy fingerpicking, but you can adapt it to alternate picking or other styles. Some fingerings may be adjusted for better flow.

THE GOSPEL SHOUT RUN

The following groove has its roots in African-American slave spiritual dances and is a foundation of gospel, soul, R&B, blues, and jazz. The "shout" is a very fast double-time groove on the drums accompanied by a chromatic bass line. This is a bass line where many of the notes are a half step apart. The root of the chord comes around on the first eighth note of the measure. Below are two shout runs based on an E root at the 7th fret of the 3rd string. Once you've got them smooth and solid, try each run in other keys on the neck.

*Start with 4 on repeats

CODE SIXTEEN TWENTY-FIVE

The pattern below shows a I–vi–ii–V ("one-six-two-five") progression in the key of E, which would be E–C#min–F#min–B7. This type of progression shows up all the time in jazz-influenced music. The roots are on beats 1 and 3 of each bar. In between the roots are *chromatic approach tones*, which lead into the root notes from a half step below or above. Once you have this pattern, you can move it to any key.

RUNNING IN PLACE

Below are a couple of chromatic patterns to keep things interesting when you have to stay
on one root for a long time in a song. You can also make progressions out of these patterns
by moving them around to new roots. These examples are good for working on your alternate
picking. Try hard to keep the volume level even from note to note. Also keep an eye on the left-
hand fingering. In the A example, you'll use your 4th finger for the E note on the 7th fret of the
3rd string so that your 3rd finger will be free to grab the B on the 7th fret of the 4th string.
In the B example, there are some small position shifts, including the move of the 1st finger from
fret 5 to fret 4, as well as some stretches.

DISCO OCTAVES

Why is it that the movie *Saturday Night Fever* is shown so often on Friday night TV? While you
ponder this question, you can work on your disco octaves. The first pattern climbs up from an
A root on the 5th fret of the 4th string. The second pattern starts at the A, then jumps down
and climbs back up. Try to make the low roots full and fat, and the octaves staccato and punchy.
These are great to slap and pop, too, if you're into that sort of thing.

FUN WITH THE ROOT, 5TH, AND 6TH

The two chord tones that are used the most in bass lines are the root and 5th (see page 28 for more on chord tones). If you've had enough of roots and 5ths but you still want your bass line to fit a major chord, try adding the 6th into the mix as a *passing tone* (a non-chord tone placed melodically between two chord tones). You can create bass lines with a lot of motion and energy by using the root, 5th, and 6th of a chord. A famous and driving example of this is the bass line in Otis Redding's R&B classic "I Can't Turn You Loose," which was also performed by The Blues Brothers. Below is a pattern that has some of that spirit on a G chord and a C chord. The chord tones are labeled. You may need to *barre* (lay a left-hand finger flat across two or more adjacent strings at the same fret) your 1st finger on two strings for some of the pattern; there are some quick string switches.

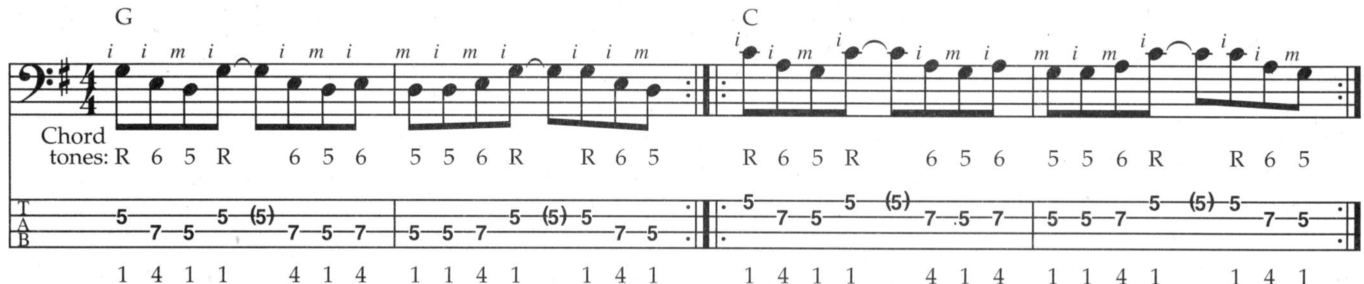

MORE ATTITUDE WITH THE ROOT, 5TH, AND ♭7TH

Another note you can add to the root/5th mix is the ♭7th. With these three notes, you can create lines that will work with minor chords, as well as major chords with a bluesy tonality. Some examples include The Doors' "Break on Through," Bob Marley's "Lively Up Yourself," and the intro to Ray Charles' "What'd I Say." Following are four patterns using the root (A), 5th (E), and ♭7th (G) of an A7 or A Minor chord. Try them on other chords, too.

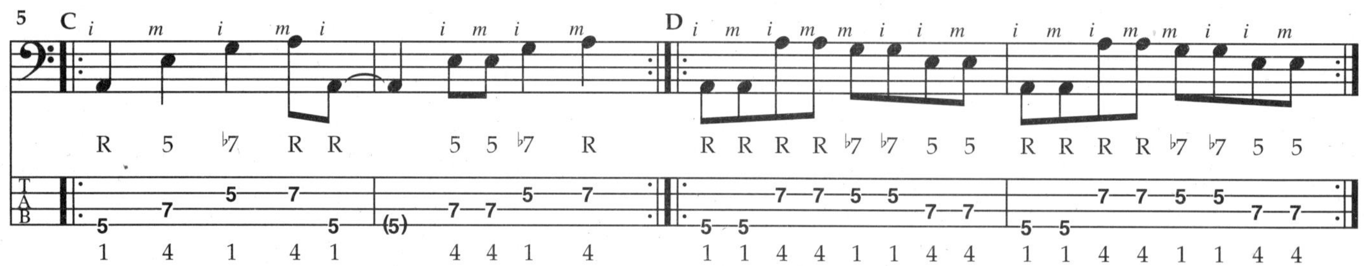

TURNING IT UP TO TEN(THS)

Playing full chords on the bass is fun, but it can be hard to distinguish the harmony of a bunch of very low notes all piled up together. Bass players who want to harmonize a line will often use the interval of a 10th because the notes are spread apart. A 10th is simply an octave plus a 3rd. 10ths can be major or minor, just like 3rds. When you play a 10th, you might visualize it as a 3rd that has been spread apart by an octave. Below are the fingerings for a major 10th on G and a minor 10th on A. The low note is the root, and the high note is still referred to as the "3rd," because that is its function in the harmony. Sound the strings by using your thumb on the 4th string and *i* or *m* on the 1st string.

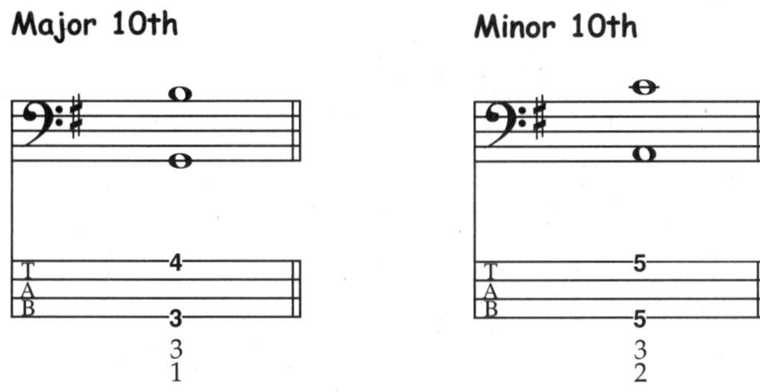

WORKING WITH A G MAJOR SCALE HARMONIZED IN 10THS

Exercise A below is a full G Major scale on the 4th string that has been harmonized with 10ths on the 1st string. The scale degrees of the roots have been identified, as well as the order of major and minor 10ths used to harmonize the scale. Notice that the 3rd finger of the fretting hand guides the hand up and down the 1st string, while the roots are played by the 1st finger on a major 10th, and the 2nd finger on a minor 10th. Exercise B is a sequence to help you move around in the harmonized major scale without losing your place.

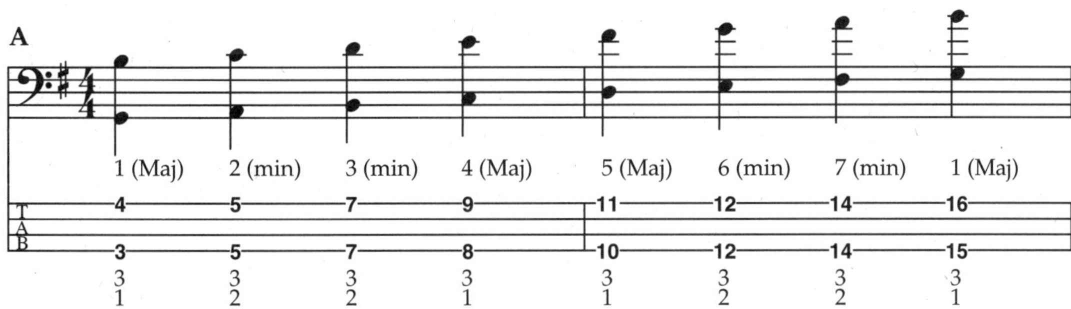

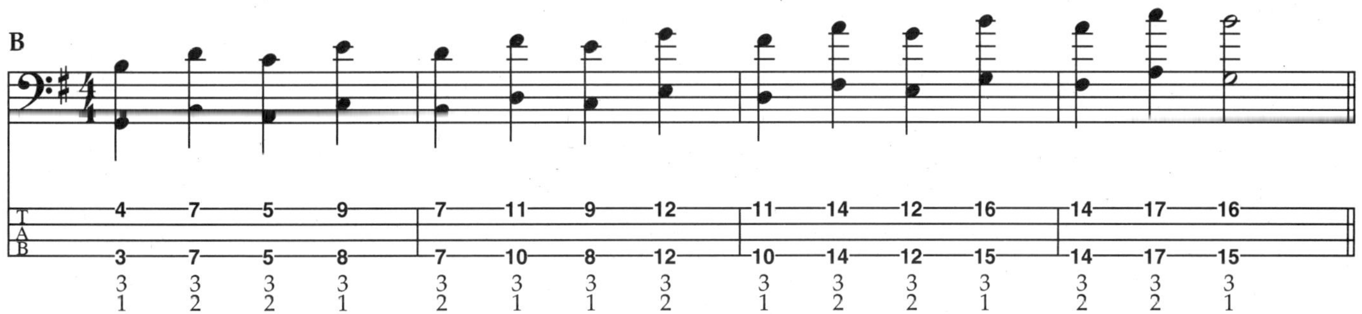

SPECIAL EFFECTS THAT BENEFIT FROM MINDLESS COUCH PRACTICE

There many kinds of practice situations, and there are many (many, many) things to practice. The trick is to match up the right practice goals to the right situations. If you're trying to take advantage of some time where it's too distracting to focus on music or compositional goals (like now, when you're on the couch reading and flicking popcorn at the cat), look for things to practice that are purely technical and need lots of time to develop. Here are some examples.

VIBRATO

Vibrato is something you need in your playing; it represents your own unique and personal expressive voice on the instrument. Vibrato is a slight change in pitch on a particular note, where the change oscillates back and forth with the original note (or another change in pitch). Most styles of vibrato on the bass are sharp, meaning the pitch change is made by bending or moving the string to make the note slightly sharp. Because of this, you have to be careful with your choices of when and how much vibrato to use. A loud, unstable or out-of-tune bass note can actually make a whole band sound out-of-tune. A true vibrato is accomplished by raising and lowering the pitch of the note by an equal amount above and below the center pitch. You can only reliably accomplish this on a fretless or upright bass.

Not everybody spends a lot of time practicing finger vibrato, because it is a complex muscle movement that develops slowly over time. This means you could practice it for 5 or 10 minutes today and not necessarily notice that it's getting better, which is frustrating. Practice it every day for a couple of weeks, however, and you'll feel a change. Some player's signature sound takes years to develop.

Couch time is an ideal time to practice vibrato. Just practice moving the string on the fret with your left-hand fingers. It can actually be helpful to distract your conscious mind with the TV or the stereo while you do this. Make it a purely physical thing, just sit there and do it. Take away the demanding, goal-oriented part of your mind and just allow yourself to get used to the motion.

There are many techniques for vibrato, but they all involve moving the string against the fret, either up-and-down (as in string bending), or back-and-forth (the way a cellist or classical guitarist might do it). A slow, narrow vibrato can help sustain a note if you need to hold it a long time and it starts to fade. Watch your favorite players and imitate their techniques and sounds. Experiment with changing the width and speed of your vibrato. Soon you'll develop your own collection of sounds to work into your playing.

GHOST NOTES

Often inhabiting old inns and prisons, these are the kinds of notes that teams of "paranormal investigators" on cable TV attempt to talk to and capture on night vision video. Not really. Ghost notes are muted, often unpitched notes that are played before or between the main notes of the bass line. Sometimes they are called "dead notes" (which is really not much of an improvement for the notes if you think about it). Ghost notes are part of the groove, and as such they fall in specific rhythmic spots. They give more depth, motion, and character to the groove.

The easiest way to approach ghost notes is to think about how one person might count off a tune: "One and Two and Three and Four," while another might go: "a-One and a-Two and a-Three and a-Four." Those "a's" fall in the same spots where ghost notes could occur.

There are several ways to execute ghost notes on the bass. Here are a few.

- **Left-hand-finger-muted ghost notes:** This type of ghost note usually happens just before a main (non-ghost) note. Using the same finger that's going to play the main note, place the finger on the note to be played without pressing the note down. Pluck the string with the muted note, then press down the main note and pluck again. Keep thinking "a-One, a-Two."

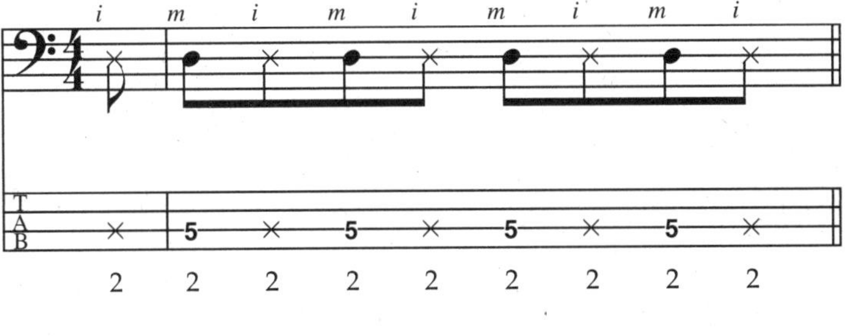

- **Adjacent-string ghost notes:** You can also play a ghost note on a string that is adjacent to the main note. You can either let the ghost note be an open string, or you can damp it with an unused finger on your left hand. Try it with both the higher and lower adjacent strings.

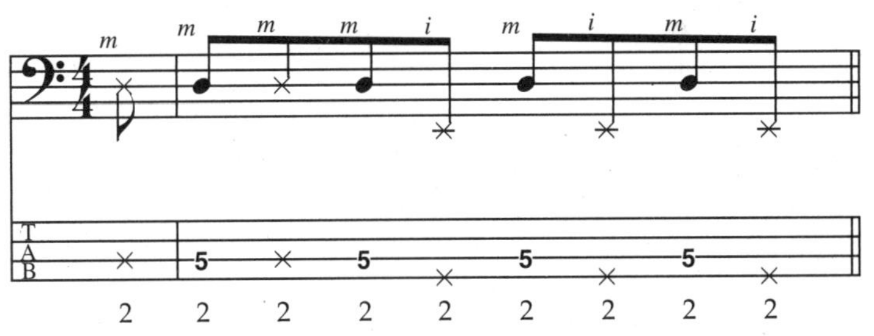

- **Open-string-pull-off ghost notes:** These ghosts usually happen after the main note. Play the main note, then pull-off to the open string for the ghost note, which is then followed by another main note. This sound is used by upright jazz players (as are the other techniques). It takes practice to keep the open strings subdued enough so that they don't take over the sound. The main note is shown accented, to remind you to give it emphasis. This technique may sound better in some keys than others, due to the open strings.

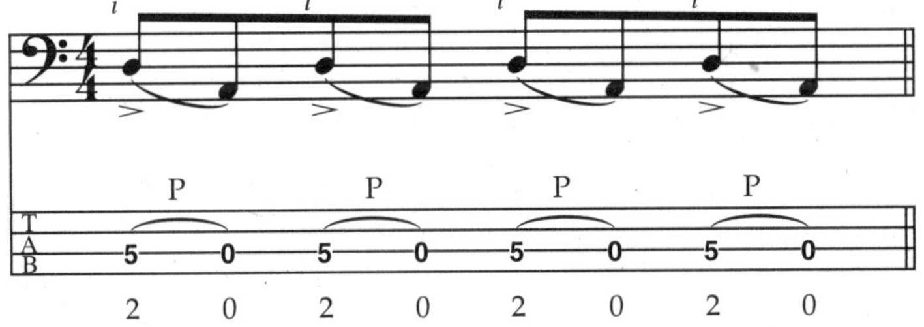

You can practice inserting ghost notes into many of the exercises in this book. Try them on different beats in the bar and using different fingers.

THE COUCH POTATO FUNBOOK: IDEAS FOR INTERACTIVE PRACTICE

The electric bass loves the television. Just think of all the TV themes that are built on a fantastic bass line! Here are some suggestions for how you can have a less zombie-like interaction with your friend the television. Of course, you could also turn off the TV and join a band, but that would be crazy.

COMPOSE AN INSTANT SOUNDTRACK

The most obvious use of your instrument while watching the tube is to make up a new soundtrack for whatever show you happen to be watching. This can be difficult if the show is already full of music, but a little careful selection of programming can lead to a lot of fun.

Programs that have lots of empty space for your new soundtrack music:

- **Certain cop/detective shows:** Particularly ones with the words "Law" and "Order" in the title.
- **Old movies from the '30s and '40s:** Specifically the less famous ones that didn't spend as much money on music.
- **Silent movies:** Whole bands have erupted in the 21st century that go out to venues and make up new music for silent movies. There are still classic film channels that show these regularly.
- **Instructional programs:** Cooking and home improvement shows, hunting and fishing shows, and public educational programming all have wide open spaces that are just crying out for your musical genius.
- **News channels:** Seriously, what news program couldn't be improved by your musical commentary?
- **Soap operas, courtroom shows, afternoon talk shows:** The list goes on and on...

Soundtracks are full of elements that are suited to specific types of situations. Here are some of the soundtrack elements you could work into your playing.

- **Stingers:** These are chords or themes that punctuate moments of excitement. Stingers are a great way to practice new or weird chords and can make a show much funnier or scarier than it is.
- **Transitions/bumpers:** This is the music that is used to get from scene to scene, or to play the show out to a commercial break. Hit the mute button early, and be the band!
- **Leitmotifs:** Back in the big opera days, composers such as Richard Wagner would write short musical themes for each character to capture their essence and introduce them when they came on stage. These themes are called *leitmotifs* (pronounced "light mow teef"). Writing leitmotifs for characters can be a particularly fun way to interact with otherwise soul-crushing reality shows.
- **Chase scenes:** There is always lots of room in a soundtrack for you to solo or groove. Of course, you'll have to figure out what key the music is in, which must be done by using your ear to first determine the root note—the note on your bass that seems strongest, or seems to best match the music in the soundtrack. This will take some trial and error and some searching, but, with time and practice, you will improve. Next, you have to determine if the key is major or minor. Starting on the root note, try a minor pentatonic scale and then a major pentatonic scale. The one that doesn't seem to clash with the soundtrack is the one to use.

"HI BOB"—THE BASS EDITION

Way back in the 1970s there was a wildly popular TV show called "The Bob Newhart Show." The show's popularity in reruns spawned an impromptu parlor game known as "Hi Bob." Whenever anybody greeted Mr. Newhart on the show with the words "Hi Bob," viewers would take a sip of their favorite beverage (an herbal tea or a cranberry spritzer, perhaps.)

You could adapt this game to your bass and save yourself a fortune in swizzle sticks. Just take your favorite show and pick out a catch phrase. Whenever it is uttered by a character on the show, the first person in the room to dash off a gospel shout run or a series of disco octaves wins the round. For example, if you're watching a home improvement show, you could play a run or a bass line every time somebody says "dated cabinets." You'll get a lot of practice this way.

IMITATION GAMES

Here are some games you can only play when you're the only person in the house. This will be so irritating to your friends and family (unless they are all avant-garde musicians) that you may become homeless if you try this when they're around. These games are great for freeing you up from physical habits and giving new inspiration to your music.

The object of the game is to imitate what you hear or see on the screen. Here are some variations:

- **Ear-Training Imitation:** Anytime you hear a bit of music on the TV show, try to play it back right after you hear it. You could try to get it as correct as possible, or just imitate the basic musical shape and attitude of the thing. The more correctly you can reproduce it, the more you are training your ears for melody, harmony, and rhythm.

- **Speech Imitation:** As you watch a show or movie, try to imitate the speech of the characters with your instrument. Imitate the rhythms, the rises and falls of pitch and inflection, and the intensity of emotion. This is especially fun if you're watching something that would be mind-numbingly stupid if you weren't covering up all the dialogue with your playing.

- **Improvisation from Visual Inspiration:** Try to interpret the action on the screen by playing your instrument. This is not quite the same as coming up with an instant soundtrack. This improv exercise will probably sound much wilder and weirder. If someone is strolling, play your idea of "strolling." If you see someone chopping zucchini, interpret that on the instrument. Alternatively, you could try to imitate the emotions of characters, or even the colors and lighting that the director has used.

CONCLUSION

As you have discovered, there are many ways to take advantage of your vegging-out time in front of the TV. These times are actually perfect opportunities to work on and develop technical skills that might otherwise be a bit tedious to work on if your mind wasn't occupied by something else. As mentioned in the Introduction, many of the exercises in this book require some preparation. It might take you a little time to learn a new pattern or technique. But once you get it down, it will take very little thought to sit there and noodle away—building your speed, agility, and finger independence while staying caught up on your favorite TV shows. Hey, you're also spending quality time with the person (or persons) at the other end of the couch (maybe not so much...). Anyway, the point is, it's not always a bad thing to be a couch potato. Have some fun learning your instrument; there are opportunities for growth and development in places you least expect!